# The Battle Axe for Emotional Healing

Catherine Ewing-Booker

C.U.P
Creative Unity Pu

*The Battle Axe for Emotional Healing*



ISBN 978-0-9822796-4-9

Cover Design: Donna Osborn Clark at CreationsByDonna@gmail.com

Layout and Interior Design: www.CreationByDonna.com

Editing: Timothy G. Green at Inkaissance: inkaissance@gmail.com

Published by: Creative Unity Publishing

# References

The following versions of The Holy Bible were used and cited within the pages of this book. These versions were used randomly by the author of this book for the flow of the poetry within this book.

Online reference used www.Biblegateway.com. Bible Gateway. Web. 2014 - 2015.

King James Version (KJV)

Publisher: Public Domain

New King James Version (NKJV)



New Living Translation (NLT)



New International Version (NIV)



English Standard Version (ESV)



New American Standard Bible (NASB)



American Standard Version (ASV)

Copyright © 1901 by Public Domain

This Book is dedicated to my Lord and Savior Jesus Christ and to my father, Jeffrey Booker and mother Pearling Ewing. It is also dedicated to every person who believed in me as a person and saw past my flaws and embraced the Jesus in me. I love you and I pray God's blessings over your life.

# Acknowledgments

First off, I have to say thank you to my Father in Heaven. Daddy thank You, for giving me this gift so freely, that I did not deserve.

Lord, many do not know how I began writing poetry, so this is the perfect time to tell them. In college, I got into an argument with my college roommate. This argument led me to write mean things about her in my journal. As I was writing, a thought popped in my mind that said to pray for her. In the end, my first poem was a prayer.

The ascribable anointing fell upon me. I thank God for every friend, church member, or family member, who gave an ear to listen to my poetry. I say thank you to my sister Shante, who is my number one fan. You have encouraged me tremendously to express myself in different ways. I love you dearly. I want to acknowledge those who interceded for me.

Lord, thank you for placing strong willed, hard- working, dedicated family members in my life. Aunt Carolyn and Uncle Marcus thank you for giving us a positive outlook on life. Thank you for my friend and sister in Christ Amber Roberts. You have encouraged me to grow spiritually and have given lots of guidance in this writing process. I thank the Lord He placed you in my life. I thank God for you, and, to Anointed House of Prayer in Vincennes, Indiana. You have given me spiritual insight and you believed in me so much. You saw the gift of poetry that God has put inside me.

To my Rock family; all of you have loved me for my goofy self. You have encouraged me to write even deeper. To everyone who complimented me, invited me to worship through writing, or gave me constructive criticism, thank you so much.

To my wonderful frontline warriors; Pastor Lavon and Prophetess Shanese Dozier. To my spiritual parents, thank you. You have truly given birth to God's purpose in me. You taught me how to walk. Both of you have spoken life to my dry bones. Your loving rebukes have made me a stronger Woman of God. Thanks for letting me minister through spoken word.

I thank God for First Lady Shanese Dozier, for not only hearing God's voice, but telling me what she heard. She prophesied over me and said that God has giving me a battle Axe anointing. Jeremiah 51:20 says, "You are my battle Axe, my weapon for battle with you I shatter nations, with you I destroy kingdoms." I hope you enjoy reading what God has to say to your wounded soul.

Thank you, Lorinda Taylor for encouraging me to keep the writing process going. I would also like to thank Sharris Pitt-Going and Genevieve McGuire for interceding for my book process. I thank them for their wisdom, knowledge and guidance.

# Introduction

## Explanation of Battle Axe

Battle Axe for Emotional Healing is written for the emotionally wounded men and women who have been through life's tough issues, confused on who they are in Christ and struggling with un-forgiveness. My poems are like a battle axe tool which God uses as purifying fire to my spirit to set me free from bondage. These poetic words are like a two edge sword. Hebrews 4:12 says, "For the word of God is quick, and powerful, and sharper than any two-edged sword, piercing even to the dividing asunder of soul and spirit, and of the joints and marrow, and is a discerner of the thoughts and intents of the heart."

It was prophesied to me that God was making me His battle axe. The word battle axe stuck out so much I had to look this word up in scripture. I was lead to Jeremiah 51:20-23 that says, 'Thou art my battle axe and weapons of war: for with thee will I break in pieces the nations, and with thee will I destroy kingdoms; And with thee will I break in pieces the horse and his rider; and with thee will I break in pieces the chariot and his rider; With thee also will I break in pieces man and woman; and with thee will I break in pieces old and young; and with thee will I break in pieces the young man and the maid; I will also break in pieces with thee the shepherd and his flock; and with thee will I break in pieces the husbandman and his yoke of oxen; and with thee will I break in pieces captains and rulers."

I didn't realize the gift of writing poetry was one of the many weapons God was using, through me, to tear down the enemy camp. Through this revelation came the title of this book: The Battle Axe for Emotional Healing. We are Gods warriors, His divine battle axes who are called to be swift, sharp, strong, and powerful. I believe God wants us to quit looking at our insignificance and inabilities and to stop making excuses for them! It is time to be the battle axe that God ordained us to be. Look through the eyes of victory, the eyes of Jesus and realize it's time for war!

Table of Contents

# Emotional Healing

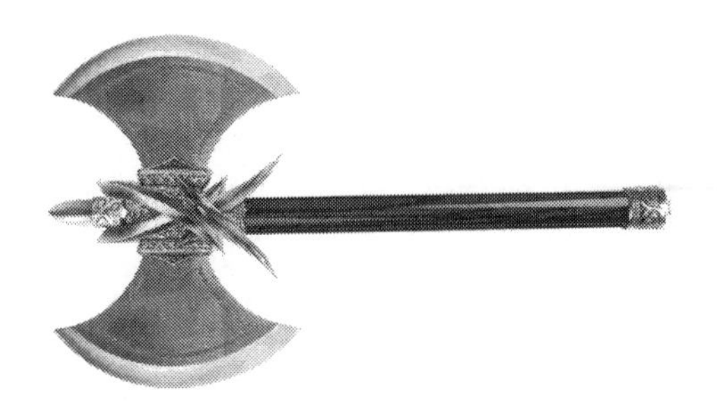

# Battle Axe I

## I Desire To Make You Whole Again

**Galatians 5:1 (NIV)*: It's for freedom that Christ has set us free stand firm then do not let yourselves be burden again to the yoke of slavery.***

This Poem addresses the issue of un-forgiveness and the need to forgive ourselves for past failures and bad decisions that one could have made, as well as the need to forgive others ranging from simple to traumatic. Holding on to un-forgiveness is a stronghold in the mind that causes health issues, such as high blood pressure, heart attacks, and stress related issues, including mental, sleep, and eating disorders. Because we are spiritual beings, we cannot deal with the issues of our heart by substituting this pain with drugs, alcohol, materialism, pride, or self blame. It's a matter of the heart that only God can restore, if one just releases it and gives it to God.

## I DESIRE TO MAKE YOU WHOLE AGAIN

Your heart is a clogged up sewer full of negative emotions that need to be released in forgiveness.

Forgiveness is surrendering your rights to get revenge. It's a cleansing action that produces emotional, physical and spiritual healing.

Because your crushed spirit is paralyzed, you cannot move properly into your destiny; neither can you possess the land of milk and honey.

Your mind is a birdcage holding inside anger, frustration, bitterness, hate and pain.

This stronghold is toxic waste in your soul that produces cancer to the bones.

Un-forgiveness is a slow fade death screaming for cardiac arrest.

It's like a heart attack cutting off God's love supply; keeping it from flowing through you. One cannot truly love if one cannot truly forgive.

God wants to release you to freedom, but your emotions are strangling you to death.

Therefore, it's the reason for the chemical imbalance in your mind, because you're living in the past, still pressing rewind.

*It's for freedom that Christ has set us free stand firm then do not let yourselves be burden again to the yoke of slavery.*

Galatians 5:1 ESV

But you are a slave in bondage. Lack of Joy, lack of peace, agitated nights, night terrors, no sleep.

God is saying: I have made the Way of escape through My Son, who died on the Cross for YOU, personally.

His bloodshed as He was beaten unrecognizably, so that you can experience peace and restoration.

There is no condemnation in me,

Release yourself to freedom

Let go of un-forgiveness

Be free!

I am The Great I Am,

Clothed in Majesty.

I come to heal the broken heart and stitch up the wounds; I Am the surgeon in the room.

Let me wash you in My blood. Let Me purify your mind, let Me give you a new nature, created to be like Me; truly righteous, holy and wearing kingdom citizenship clothing.

This is My Promise to you.

So release! I want you to know that I was there when you were beaten; I was there when you were molested and I was there when you were homeless and suicidal. I was there when you were strung out on drugs. I was there when you were prostituting yourself.

I was there when people talked about you, I WAS THERE! You were not shut out of My plans.

For you are My master piece, I am the potter and you are the clay, yes you are fearfully and wonderfully made.

All your pain I allowed because your disappointments will produce promise.

All things work together for the good of those who love Me.

If you are mad at Me don't be. I desire to bless you with heavenly blessings on earth and eternally.

*Come unto me, all ye that labor and are heavy burden, you who hold on to un-forgiveness I will give you rest.*

Mathew 11:28 ESV

Take My yoke upon you and learn of Me; for I am meek and lowly in heart: and ye shall find rest unto your souls for My yoke is easy and My burden is light.

Let's have a divine exchange; your un-forgiveness for My healing to your mind, body and spirit.

God is telling you that every dead thing in you that un-forgiveness killed, including your hopes, integrity, dreams, marriage, friendships, and family; I will revive back to life.

My love is an oxygen machine, pumping vision back in you, because I desire to make you whole again.

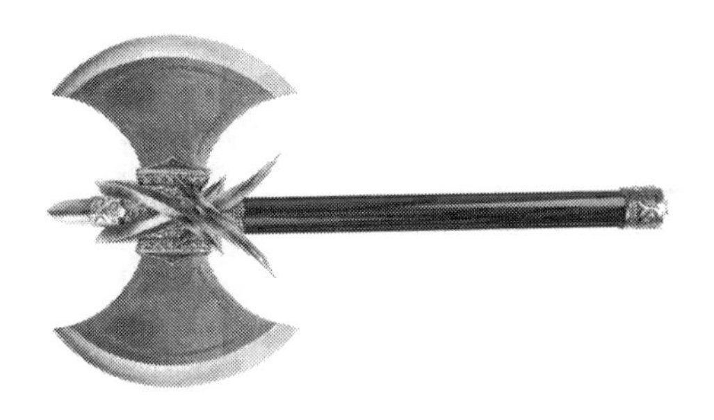

# Battle Axe 2

## Emotional Freedom

**Proverbs 28:17 (NLT)** ***A man tormented by the guilt of murder will be a fugitive till death; let no one support him.***

# EMOTIONAL FREEDOM

The mind is kidnapped by the emotional pressures of life, causing one to walk in double mindedness.

A double minded man is unstable in all his ways. Walking in mood swings of the spirit and flesh.

Out of the heart come the issues of life.

When the heart is sick it breathes inconsistency in the spiritual realm, producing spiritual bipolar that is influenced by being unstable in the mind.

Attitudes and disposition; stuck in past glory, hard to move in transition.

The matters of the heart blows like an ocean wave over the tongue, causing one to speak poisonous words in the atmosphere that infiltrates the human body and leads to spiritual death.

My emotional outbursts pulled the trigger of my tongue, releasing words like bullets in self; this is equivalent to suicidal death.

My emotions were my foundation, which was identical to quicksand. I was sinking through my issues of life, hard to stand.

My unhealthy emotions were my God; a foul stench in God's nostrils, because He who knows what to do and don't do… it is sin.

Sin separates us from the Father and as I continually walked in UN forgiveness and offense I was disconnected with Him.

I worshipped my pain instead of the painkiller Jesus; He is my medication.

He wants to be the chemical that brings balance in your mind.

Kicking at the door of my heart were the spirits of rejection, the perception of favoritism, mental disorder, envy, and false accusation. This is the opposite of love, for love keeps no records of wrong.

Looking through the eyes of the stronghold of my imagination created an eye disease. For all I saw was deception, false perception, and false reality.

My appetite has been set on eating until I'm fully connected with a ministry; instead of on Christ.

*A man tormented by the guilt of murder will be a fugitive till death; let no one support him.*

Proverb 28:17 NLT

Emotional bondage produces a murdering spirit.

This murdering spirit looks through the eyes of offense, manipulation, jealousy, rage, self pity, and gossip.

Let no one support him says the Lord, for you are disconnected from Me and no you cannot connect with the ministry first for that will become your God.

Now you are not ready for a leadership position. You will sit until you humble yourself and let Me heal those wounds; for running after other gods produces sorrow. My beautiful daughter, my vase, you are on The Potter's wheel where there are cracks I must heal.

Anything broken I can mend again.

Trust in My hands, for I am an artist and you are My masterpiece.

He who pursues righteousness and love finds life, honor, and prosperity.

Lord, endow our hearts with Your wisdom and give understanding to our minds so that we don't give in to false perceptions.

Cleanse our eyes from spiritual glaucoma. Lord, change us in the midst of adversity so that our spirit man bleeds humility, as we face many kinds of trials.

I know that the testing of our faith develops perseverance; perseverance must finish its work so that we may be mature and complete not lacking anything.

My God is purging the body from co- dependency, from needing people more than Him, from attention seeking behaviors and pride.

Lord I surrender; I am trading in my emotional pain for emotional deliverance.

I am trading in my pity party for my victory. Oh well, even if it's just me and God.

I am done trying to fit in, when my God created me to stand out.

I am done trying to be in a church position when my God called me to the community.

God has called us to humility.

Humility is suffering like Jesus suffered on the cross. He was a King, the son of God, but considered Himself nothing.

He took the nature of a servant.

Humility takes a demotion, while pride promotes self on a man-made platform; verbalizing gifts and callings with no anointing.

Prideful arms are wrapped around arrogance, self entitlement and insecurities; strangling the throat of the spirit.

God chooses those who are poor in the eyes of the world to be rich in faith and to inherit the Kingdom He promised to those who love Him.

If you feel lonely, or rejected; left out and over-looked please know this. In God eyes, it's you he chooses, for you are poor and there is need for you in the Kingdom.

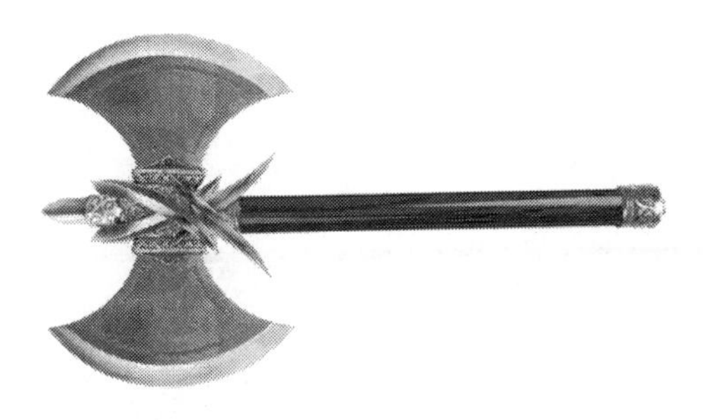

# Battle Axe 3

## Arise

**2 Chronicles 7:14 (ESV)** ***If my people who are called by my name will humble themselves, pray and seek my face and turn from their wicked ways, I will heal their land, my eyes will be open and ears attentive to every prayer made in this place***

## ARISE

I speak to the dead bones in America.

The scattered bones across the valley that are dried out by rebellion; a betrayed heart, sickness, worldly possessions, idleness, a broken heart, poverty, depression and a religious spirit.

God says I want your HEART! I don't want your money, talents, or praises.

I want the willing vessel who will say, "Yes."

A vessel that has a repentant, converted, and submitted heart… I want their worship.

The righteous prayer is like the aroma of rose petals to My nostrils.

Why are you giving Me trash as your love offering to Me?

Why are you negotiating a deal with Me about your sin that you desire to hold on to so tightly?

Give Me what I ask for; the skeletons hidden in your closet.

Like Abraham was willing to kill Isaac, the promise child, AM I WORTH IT? AM I WORTH IT?

Am I worth more than the sin you cling so tightly to?

I want to take those plastic beads and give you diamonds, but you are stuck on short term gratification, things that are fake, things that are lifeless.

In these last days hearts have been bound by a Judas spirit, a spirit of betrayal.

Why are you betraying Jesus for the decay of this world?

*If my people who are called by my name will humble themselves, pray and seek my face and turn from their wicked ways, I will heal their land, my eyes will be open and ears attentive to every prayer made in this place.*

2 Chronicles 7:14 ESV

*God says dry bones listen to the word of the Lord! I am going to put breath into you and make you alive again. I will put flesh and muscle on you and cover you with skin I will put breathe into you and you will come to life.*

Ezekiel 37:4-6 TLB

We are moving from being dry bones to becoming God's great army.

We are being resurrected to life in Jesus.

God says you will be My people and I will be your God.

*When I cleanse you from your sins, I will repopulate your city and the ruin will be rebuilt, the field that used to lie empty and desolate in plain view of everyone will again be formed and when I bring you back America, people will say this former waste land is now like the Garden of Eden! Lord Transform America, pick up their bow down head, Lord repair this broken city.*

Ezekiel 36:36 NLT

Let us be unified in You as a community.

Let us be united in the spirit; binding ourselves with peace.

Now that our dead bones have been revived by His spirit, let us American, authentic, born again Christians imitate God in everything we do because we are His children.

We are His special possession.

Let's be a city on our knees; humbly crying out for the oppression of our country and those affected by it.

Let us be a nation that loves JESUS by our action, because apart from Jesus, we can do nothing.

Jesus is our total fulfillment. Jesus is the Restoration this nation needs.

It is time to prepare the way for the King to come visit America.

The Church in America has become a stumbling block to the world.

Eighty percent claims to be Christian, but only 20 percent are living it.

This is a form of Godliness, but denying the power thereof.

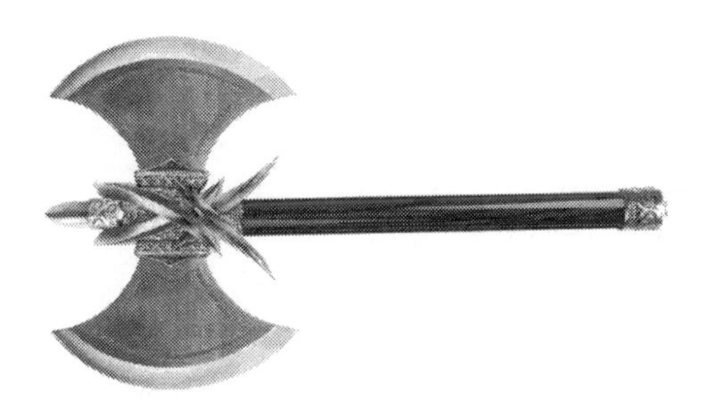

# Battle Axe 4

## God Knows

**Psalm 127:3 (NLT)** ***Children are a gift from the Lord; they are a reward from him.***

## GOD KNOWS

Is it meant to be?

Or not meant to be?

The things that I cannot imagine,

Or don't see,

My Heavenly Father sees,

A long story short, only God knows what joy brings.

I can't provoke the future, or willingly rush for it to come because maybe what I dream ain't meant to be.

If I see a dark path on this rocky road, shall I fall off?

I can't predict the future because only God knows.

The love I regurgitate from my heart to the one I love... Is it meant to be or not meant to be?

Let the future unfold.

But ah, I can't predict the future because only God knows.

The fetus that developed from the semen you delivered in my swimming pool of lust.

The milk that develops in my body is surely food for the fetus's soul.

Is it meant to be or not meant to be?

But, um, I can't predict the future because only God knows.

I sit and wonder how will I deal with life?

I'm in college; I can't afford a baby. I can barely afford an education; it's like a dream.

That's why I ask is it meant to be, or not meant to be?

With life I cannot afford the struggle.

But, um, I can't predict the future because only God knows

Is it unnatural to feel complication with my pregnancy?

Is it unnatural to feel the beauty of a baby moving in my body?

Is it unnatural to feel a bond, but all in one? Is it meant to be, or not?

I can't predict the future because only God knows.

I am built up with happiness, but also broken down with fear. I wanted to be in love, not just give it up.

I don't want this baby, but then again I do. Neither abortion nor a miscarriage is what I want to go through.

I don't want to endure the emotional scars, so God I will give my baby up for adoption to You.

You can father this baby with Your unconditional love as You teach me skills to be a mother.

Your word says in Psalms 127:3 NLT *Children are a gift from the Lord. They are a reward from him.*

I know that I created this baby out of wedlock, but I know that this baby is not a mistake. When a man and woman come together sexually, it biologically makes since for a woman to get pregnant.

Lord, I ask for forgiveness and I move on, in destiny, as I give birth to a gracious reward from above.

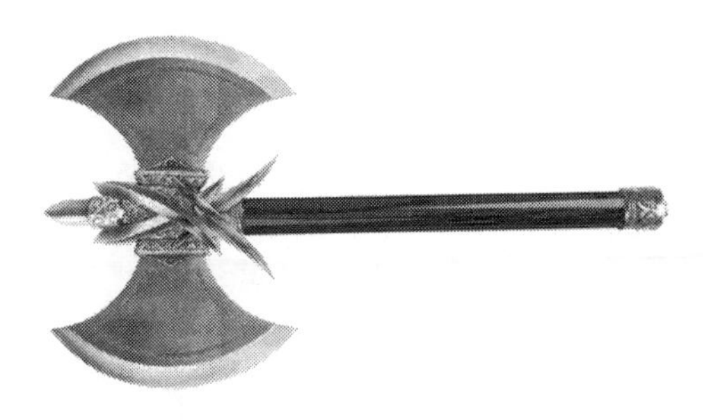

# Battle Axe 5

## Ugly Duckling To Swan

**Psalm 45:11 (NIV)** ***The king is enthralled with your beauty***

## UGLY DUCKLING TO SWAN

I have been walking with God for a very long time and I still wrestle with self-doubt, lack of trust, and uncertainty.

This is a head on collision; a giant that I must defeat.

As I go thru transformation, He is redefining my beauty while loving me unconditionally.

Jesus is pulling the scab away from my insecurities. This process is painful, but I'll walk away with a limp in victory.

Ever since I was a little girl I always felt like an ugly duckling that was picked on and defeated because of my appearance.

Insecurity, consummated with rejection, gives birth to an ugly duckling that longs the want to be accepted, loved, and appreciated.

I was the girl with low self-esteem, buck teeth, and wrinkled shoes that came to school looking filthy and dirty.

My identity was rooted in how people viewed me as pretty.

I was the spotted duckling that compared me to many; looking for the answer to beauty…

Not feeling like I measured up.

I started not to care about how I looked; not even my hair.

I didn't feel good enough so I gave up.

My self -worth had eyes that looked for assurance.

It had legs that ran after the approval of man.

A mouth that ate the sweet lies of the enemy,

A nose that sniffed after the scent of fulfillment,

Ears that searched for the sound of love…

My self-worth continued to run empty.

I felt like an eagle with a broken wing; a scorpion with no sting, a drug addict looking for an identity.

I've tried to wear popularity as makeup to cover up the scars of being bullied physically and emotionally.

I had no confidence in me because I paid more attention to my weaknesses instead of my strength

My thoughts were deeply rooted in insecurities, so I began to prostitute my body for a low payment of love.

I had been sold a dream,

Been sold a lie…

I had been captured in human trafficking; a sex slave sold into sexual immorality.

I pleased people just to like me. I compromised just to fit in and denied Christ for homosexuality.

I have smelled like dead flesh of possessiveness, controlling, and demanding behaviors. It gave off an aroma in the atmosphere that stemmed from being insecure.

Its voice whispers in a passive aggressive tone, "I can't take the thought of losing you, so I will wrap you in my chain of bondage so you can feel what I feel. I want to trust that you won't hurt me, but that means I have to put my guard down.

I will hurt you before you hurt me because I can't get hurt again.

I know this is psychologically damaging.

Anger and rejection were the soldiers who guarded my heart from embracing the wholeness of Christ completely. In essence, I was pushing away all positive relationships and stability.

"What is your definition of who I am?" asked Beauty.

The scared duckling replied,

"Beauty, I have an ought against you.

For so long I felt so betrayed by you.

I felt like you left me out your presence.

You were the mask I always wanted to wear, but felt rejected.

So over time, I embraced my own definition of beauty that says,

'My beauty is my hair

My beauty is my eyes

My beauty is my body'

I'm the duckling that let man and the world, define me."

Beauty, with tears in her eyes, looked down at the duckling and said,

*The king is enthralled with your beauty* (Psalm 45:11 NIV)

*Indeed, the very hairs on your head is numbered don't be afraid; you are worth more than many sparrows*

Luke 12:7 NIV

"I give you the keys to release be free!

When God created you I was not a mask, but rather the skin He used to cover your flesh and bone.

I was the breath He breathed into you to become alive. I was the eyes He looked through when He said, "Let us make man in our image." God the Father, Son and Holy Spirit, along with me, are one in unity.

Insecurities and false perceptions of me became a burn mark that caused your skin to be scarred.

Instead of walking in Jesus fully, you began to walk in false identity.

Behold, old things have passed away, for we are a new creation and you now can embrace true security.

In Christ alone you are redeemed, refreshed, and restored.

You are found, forgiven, free...

You are chosen, chastised; a child of God and seated in a heavenly realm.

*For we are God workmanship created in Christ Jesus to do good works which he has prepare in advance for us to do.*

Eph. 2:10 NIV

Your identity is not in your titles, possession or the opinion of others.

But, in God you have power, praise and dominion.

Tell yourself it is no longer I who live but Christ who lives in me.

The King is enthralled with your beauty.

He is your assurance, confidence and hope. Let Him be the rock you stand on as a foundation that is unshaken and secure with certainty.

So duckling, know that I am also the treasure God has placed in you.

I am the heartbeat to the swan that dwells inside of you."

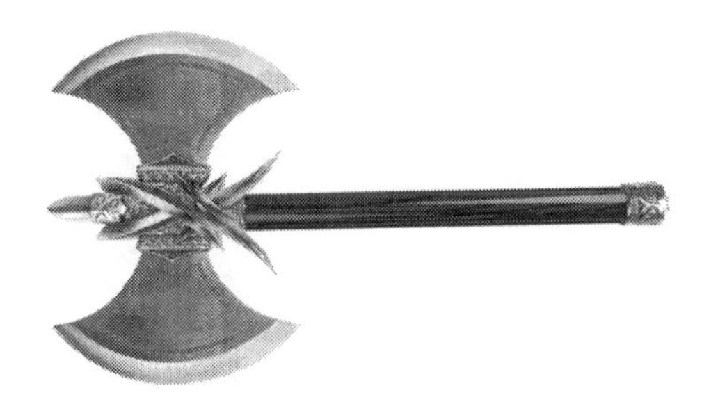

# Battle Axe 6

## The Bait Of Loneliness

**Isiah 40:31 (TLB)** ***But they that wait upon the Lord shall renew their strength; they shall mount up with wings as eagles; they shall run, not be weary; and they shall walk, and not faint.***

# THE BAIT OF LONELINESS

See, my body is craving warmth, and the fulfillment to be romanticized and nurtured.

Like fingers that pull the strings on a guitar, it's like the deep void that pulls on the strings of my heart; playing a tune that turns the voice of loneliness on.

The voice of loneliness serenades my sexually abused wounds; awakening those childhood memories. It sings to my need for attention relationally.

Your beautiful voices keeps me in a daze as I day dream and fantasize on the false possibilities of you and I. These thoughts bring me warmth and make me feel cozy.

As my mind listens to the melody of my heart, it was you loneliness, who tried to lead me astray into old habits, patterns and mindsets.

I see that you have been trying to confuse my emotions to want the ungodly, abominable and unimaginable.

I have self-medicated myself with the lust of my hand, mind, and eyes; yet I'm still empty. Loneliness is trying to ambush my spirit like a bull dozer.

I'm zapped of strength because I've chased after love in all the wrong places. Places that will never fill my void, but rather leave me dry and infected with erosion, deception and pride.

I've been dating my mind of fantasy for too long! I'm turning the radio station from loneliness to waiting. I'm singing a new song. Everything I want and desire is all in God's timing.

Waiting and loneliness are two definitions that fight for a human's destiny, purpose and fulfillment.

Waiting is what God has called us to do while loneliness is the bait that Satan uses to draw us away from the well of the living water; the word of God.

Waiting argues righteously with loneliness. It states to loneliness, "You are a harmful and deadly drug that is swallowed heavily by many.

You keep them confused with reality and the broken spirit of the unhealed. You have those who are emotionally healed debating their deliverance and the selfish continue living in pity, as the grieved grieve improperly.

Loneliness, you are connected to depression like bones are connected to tendons.

You are connected to sexual immorality like vines rooted in the ground.

You are connected to bitterness, jealousy, envy, rejection and anger like wheels connected to a car."

Waiting is the cloak of warmth that God uses.

People of God we cannot despise the article of clothing that God uses for our warmth, protection, and guidance.

Trust in the Lord with all your heart and lean not on your own understanding.

There is wisdom is waiting!

Inside, waiting is discipline of the mind, body, emotion and will.

*But they that wait upon the Lord shall renew their strength; they shall mount up with wings as eagles; they shall run, not be weary; and they shall walk, and not faint.*

Isiah 40:31 TLB

*Let none that wait on you be ashamed*

Psalm 25:3 NSAB

His word says He will not withhold any good things from those He love.

Love God with your waiting; worship God with being a glory builder.

Waiting is trusting in God during the good bad and ugly.

Look at your past, your failures, your defeats, and every familiar spirit and shout, "I'm not giving up any territory! Lord, let my life be a sponge that You use to ring out Your glory."

Patience is a virtue that causes you to surrender to God best while passing the test of faith.

When we rush God, we end up eating rotten leftovers from a trash can because we are walking in a dark kitchen of our mind and confuse the trash can with the refrigerator of light.

Oh, how long will you continue to let loneliness sing you sweet lullabies?

Every note you cling to is the enemy's voice in disguise.

Worship while you wait.

*Wait on the Lord; be of good courage, and He shall strengthen your heart; wait I say on the Lord.*

Psalm 27:14 NKJV

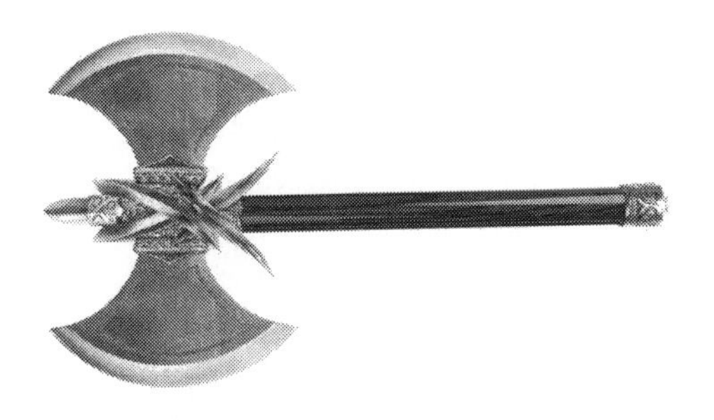

# Battle Axe 7

## The Forbidden Fruit

**1 COR.6:19-20 (NKJV)** ***Or do you not know that your body is a temple of the Holy Spirit within you, whom you have from God? You are not your own, for you were bought with a price. So glorify God in your body.***

## FORBIDDEN FRUIT

You have clothed me with friendship.

You have kept me warm when I felt naked.

You were a friend in my discomfort.

When I went through that painful divorce, it was You who ran to my door.

When my loved one died, You were the first person I called.

When I cried, You wiped the tears from my eyes.

You cheered me up when I was feeling lonely.

When I was bored You talked with me freely.

You filled my void when I felt empty.

Our friendship made me emotionally secure.

Any insecurity I had I knew You would make me feel good.

See, we had a David and Jonathan relationship that was closely knitted together.

So, I thought, in my deceived mind I was lost.

In reality I was letting You become the God of my belly.

Food, I have been friends with you so long that I have picked up the bad habit of gluttony.

I have become a slave to your intimacy.

I have become like a drug addict strung out on the addictive chemicals in food. The heroin of refined sugar and the cocaine of sodium nitrite keep me running to restaurants like a crack house.

The love of food is my craving like a sweet tooth.

The knife of junk food is stabbing me to death; killing my spirit and resuscitating my dead flesh back to life. Therefore, my body became a living sacrifice.

My taste buds arm wrestle with self-control in an effort to fulfill the need to be pleased.

When my belly began to itch, I began to scratch it with anything sustaining.

My eyes have adapted to seeing food as Jehovah Rapha; one who heals my issues. I am captured in the arms of gluttony, enjoying the gentle kisses on my cheek, while ignoring God who wants to set me free.

I continue to walk in greed, knowing I am becoming spiritually and physically weak.

Obesity has hit America like a tsunami, causing slothfulness in the limbs of our body.

I am taking the sword of the fork to my own throat and killing myself prematurely.

*For the drunkard and the glutton will come to poverty, and slumber will clothe them with rags*

Proverb 23:21 ESV

The bible says it's the little foxes that spoil the vine.

The little foxes of pounds being gain, little by little, by consumption of deadly toxins.

It's the small thing that hinders our body viciously and causes our body to be injured by health diseases called high blood pressure, high cholesterol and diabetes.

It's the reason you cannot fulfill the call of your ministry.

You have been huffing and puffing while being depleted of energy. That has caused your mission to be incomplete.

You have been singing your body sweet lies of how you're going to exercise.

Your secret sin of gluttony brings a reproach to God.

This is not a kingdom mentality.

Gluttony is like a serpent that continues to drop seeds of doubt about God; swaying your heart to give him dominion over your temple.

Like Adam and Eve abusing their body by eating of the forbidden tree, all because they doubted God's truth and became deceived.

Our spiritual position in Christ should rule over our physical greatly.

*Or do you not know that your body is a temple of the Holy Spirit within you, whom you have from God? You are not your own, for you were bought with a price.*

1Corrinthians 6:19-20 NKJV

So, glorify God in your body.

*Let your moderation be known unto all men. The Lord is at hand*

Philippians 4:5 KJV

As I sit in an intervention session with God the Father, Jesus the Son and the Holy Spirit as Counselor; in unison say, "You need to check in to the Rehab of purification."

The rehab of fasting, praying, and exercising spiritual and physical discipline will break this yoke of bondage and build my spiritual and physical muscles.

Let my body be presented as a living sacrifice, while serving God in the Holies of Holies.

His word, along with the vitamin of Self-control, will cleanse my temple of deadly toxins that are polluting me daily.

God says submit and draw near to me; resist the devil and he will flee as you purify your heart of sin. I will greatly exalt you through your humility.

Push the plate away as it is time to surrender the delicacies like Daniel did for 10 whole days by eating fruit, vegetables and whole grain.

When rehab to wholeness gets too hard I will say:

*Set a guard, O LORD over my mouth; watch over the door of my lips! Do not let my heart incline to any evil; too busy my-self with wicked deeds in company with men who work iniquity and let me not eat of their delicacies.*

Psalms141:3-4 NKJV

*Therefore whether you (I) eat or drink or whatever (I) you do, (I will) do all to the Glory of God.*

1 Corinthians 10:31 KJV

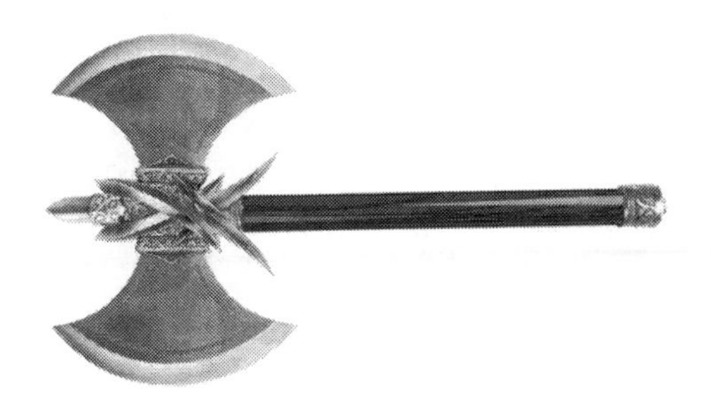

# Battle Axe 8

## Wailing Women

**Jeremiah 9:17-20 (NIV)** ***This is what the LORD Almighty says: "Consider now! Call for the wailing women to come; send for the most skillful of them. Let them come quickly and wail for us till our eyes overflow with tears and water streams our eyelids. The sound of wailing is heard from Zion. Now, O women, hear the word of the LORD; open your ears to the words of his mouth. Teach your daughters how to wail; teach one another a lament.***

# WAILING WOMEN

WOMEN LISTEN UP!

The green eyed monster of jealousy…

The blue eyed monster of envy…

The red eyed monster of comparison has kept women divided and defeated for too long!

We are so valuable to God that He has delegated us to give birth to nations. He has called us to be watchmen over this nation and our homes. We are called to fast and intercede for the lost, yet we have been eaten alive by the locust of sick emotions that keeps us competing for vanity.

We as women have been so inwardly focused that we have lost sight of the mission God has given us to be women of prayer. Our ears have been clogged up by the voice of our deceitful hearts; swaying our emotions to live in the comfort of gossiping.

He has called us to be women of mourners; instead we have become a group of whiners that grumble over petty stuff and keep us in confusion. Our eye sight has been defiled by strife and disunity.

Our cry has become silent in the ears of God. While we are in disunity, our children and men are being defeated in battle. Our cry and deep intercession should be a hedge of protection and a shield that defends the treasures placed inside of our nation's heart.

Jesus is calling the wailing women to come forth and release violent cries of grief. Let our cry be like a volcano erupting in His ear. God says, "*If they keep quiet, the stones will cry out.*" Luke19:40 NIV

*Therefore, I will wail and howl. I will go stripped and naked: I will make a wailing like the dragons, and mourning as the owls.*

Micah 1:8 KJV

Let our cry be the fingers that play the piano of Your heart; making beautiful music that serenades You and the angels in heaven. Let our cry be the instruments of brass and percussion playing in the background, as angels sing to it.

Hear our cry from the valley. God, I approach our mercy seat through the blood of Jesus and ask for forgiveness for we women who have dropped the ball in fasting and praying. God we want to become in synch with You and breathe out the emotions of the HOLY SPIRIT.

Let us connect to Your love and lose the band of wickedness of false self-image, brokenness, hurt, insecurities and low self-esteem. Let our mind be renewed and our limbs moved in action of kneeling in prayer and showing deep devotion.

Wrap us in unity; suffocating us tightly with your love. Love covers a multitude of sin and faults; let us be women working in unity to conqueror new territory.

We want to be a woman that touches God's heart with our wailing. Let our tears be like troubled water that boils over melting and molding our community.

We have been a torn body needing cosmetic surgery by the hand of GOD; cutting away the flesh of disunity, jealousy, and envy.

America has become so adulterated by Babylonian culture, that we have fell in the traps of idol worship. We have adopted a depraved mindset that causes us to blend in with the world, when we were called to stand out.

We wail because of the spiritual and moral condition of man. We want to be a spotless bride that doesn't sleep around with this immoral culture. You are calling the weeping women to unify in humility. The lower we are, the closer we are to You.

We women want to bask in Your presence through our wailing. Through our cry, let Your fragrances arise. God dance in the rain of our tears that drench Heaven.

Jesus let our heat beat in rhythm with Yours, like the beat of an African drum. Breath of God, flow though our cry. We cry out for this nation to come back to You believing in the power of the death burial and resurrection. Let our cry give birth to a pure generation focused for destiny. We fast and pray for deeper insight and wisdom, using Godly principles to govern the affairs of the kingdom. Endow us with Your Holy Ghost, so that we can purely communicate Your emotions.

# Love

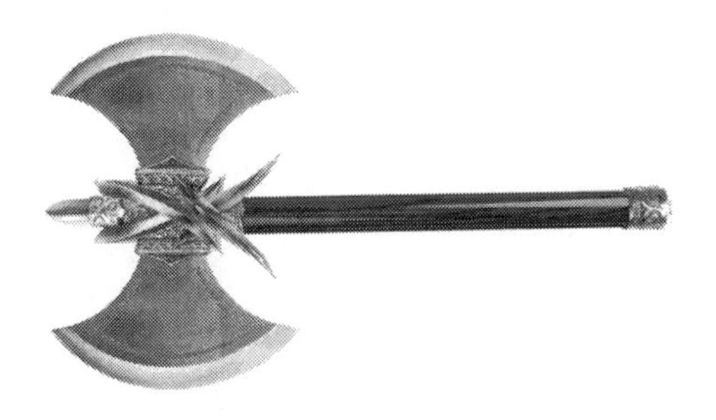

# Battle Axe 9

## Sincerely Jesus Christ

**John 14:27 (NIV)** ***I leave you peace. My peace I give you. I do not give it to you as the world gives so don't let your heart be troubled do not be afraid.***

# SINCERELY JESUS CHRIST

I will lead you in all truth.

Let Me be your virtuous love; redeeming your brokenness by scraping off your impurities, For I am The Redeemer. My love never fails; it always prevails.

Don't fight Me; this is true love.

Real love feels uncomfortable after being introduced to the wrong way for many years.

You're so beautiful to Me. I love gazing at you daily.

I enjoy being the artist of your mind and soul.

Why do you reject Me, the lover of your soul? Why do you reject Me? Do you know that I am jealous for your attention?

I will continue to pursue, but I will not beg you. You must embrace true love by the free will that I have given you.

As I whisper to your spirit while blowing My breath on your heart, I shall gloss my fingers over your mind saying, "Will choose Me, again and again."

Do not sign the divorce paper of a reprobate mind.

You have been saying yes with your mouth, but say yes with your spirit.

*I leave you peace. My peace I give you. I do not give it to you as the world gives so don't let your heart be troubles do not be afraid.*

John 14:27 NIV

Peace will not come until your yes is real with Me.

I want My branches to live, so stay connected to Me.

Oh taste and see that I am good.

I give you rest for your soul.

The question for your soul is, are you done searching? If you look up at Me I will remove the veil.

*But when a person changes and follows the Lord that covering is taking away the lord is the Spirit and where the Spirit of the Lord is liberty. Our faces then are not covered. We all show the Lord glory is being changed to be like him.*

2 Corinthian 3:17-18 ESV

This change in us brings more and more glory and it comes from the Lord who is the spirit.

With your eternal yes, our covenant is renewed with joy of happiness.

I wipe the tears from your eyes; forever you are My bride.

Again, I am the potter and you are the clay. I am the vine, you are the branches. I will lead you into all truth, for I am truth my beautiful bride.

Sincerely,

Jesus Christ

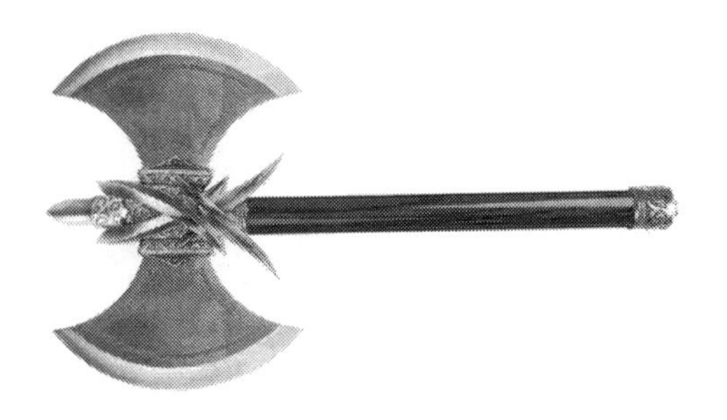

# Battle Axe 10

## Love Bares All Things

**1Corinthian 13:4-8 (NIV)** ***Love is patient, love is kind. It does not envy, it does not boast, it is not proud. It does not dishonor others, it is not self-seeking, it is not easily angered, it keeps no record of wrongs. Love does not delight in evil but rejoices with the truth. It always protects, always trusts, always hopes, always perseveres.***

***Love never fails. But where there are prophecies, they will cease; where there are tongues, they will be stilled; where there is knowledge, it will pass away.***

## LOVE BEARS ALL THINGS

Imagine love without God.

It would be hopeless, joyless, and faithless.

One who loves without God's action is done in the flesh.

What is flesh?

Flesh disappears back to dust, but our spirit lives forever.

Yes our spirit does have a home. The question is, where is yours going?

A time is coming says the Lord, when I will punish all those who are circumcised in body, but not in spirit.

Loving God with your mouth and not your heart,

Loving your neighbor with your mouth, but yet backstabbing.

Steady saying and never doing.

Love is an action!

Love is an action!

Love is not rude or jealous,

Love is not selfish,

Love is not easily provoked,

It keeps no records of wrong.

God has poured out His love into our hearts, by way of the Holy Spirit, whom He has given us.

Love is a fruit that grows on the true vine Jesus.

Love is patient and love is kind.

*Love never gives up, never loses faith, always hopeful through every circumstance.*

1Corinthian 13:4-8 NIV

Love bears all things.

I'm saying love bears all things.

Love bears all things.

*Let not the wise man glory in his wisdom, let not the rich man glory in his riches, but let him that glory in this, that he knows me, that I am the Lord which exercise loving kindness, judgment, and righteousness in earth*

Jeremiah 9:23 NIV

When riches fail you,

When financial disaster hits,

When the tornado of divorce hits, know that My love will fill the void of hardships experienced in life.

Keep your eyes on God when man lets you down, loneliness gets the best of you and heaviness tries to creep up on you.

God's love will not fail you lonely men and women, because God's love is true intimacy.

When the cares of this world are gone, love will last forever!

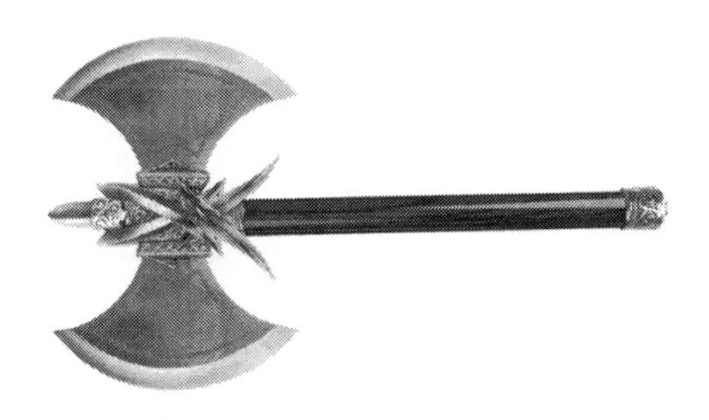

# Battle Axe II

## Love In All The Wrong Places Again

**Proverb 18:22 (HCSB)** ***A man who finds a wife finds a good thing and obtains favor from the Lord.***

## LOVE IN ALL THE WRONG PLACES

As I look at the image of my body in the mirror, I ask silently am I worth loving?

The major question is,

How can I be worth loving if I don't love myself?

How can men respect me if I don't demand respect? I search for love in all the wrong places.

I have never been loved by a true man; so when I am out in the world looking for a man to love me I don't know the signs, nor do I know this feeling.

I am a struggling woman that is determined and true love is what I am yearning.

I thought if I gave you sex with emotions attached, that your love is what I would get back.

Now I am looking stupid and sad, because you're only up to being a one night stand.

Now tears are rolling down my face, because I ended up looking for love in the wrong place again.

I thought I learned my lesson, even thought I was wise,

I thought my skin was tough for the next man who caught me by surprise.

I thought by giving men money would make them love me.

I worked hard for a man who doesn't love me back, but my mind was saying, "I'll do anything for us to be love magnets."

I flipped my last two checks on a man who I thought cared for me, but he was a faker; only draining me.

Yeah I felt crummy, but I just wanted him to be my potential hubby.

I look like a disgrace,

I looked for love in the wrong place.

I have no self-esteem and many men see this. This is how men take advantage of me.

I let it happen because my heart was crying out for love.

Why should I have anything to be guilty of?

God speaking:

Sweet heart marriage is not the goal, but building a relationship with my son, Jesus, is.

Heaven and Earth will pass away but My word stands for ever. For your Creator, Me, is Your husband and I am the King.

I can love you deeply and patiently.

I am the forgiver of your sins, and the healer of your broken heart.

It is I who will lift up your bowed head.

I want to be so intimately involved in your inner soul that you can feel My presence when I am near.

I want to bottle up your tears to pour out a blessing. Remember my queen, you need Me,

So fix your Gaze on the king.

*If then you were raised with Christ, seek those things which are above, where Christ is, sitting at the right hand of God. Set your mind on things above, not on things on the earth.*

Colossian 3:1-2 ESV

Be not tempted like Eve was in the garden by doubting my truth and eating the forbidden fruit.

Please I say, don't eat from the fruit I said no to.

*The King is enthralled with your beauty.*

Psalms 45:11 NIV

I am your restoration and peace.

I desire to make you whole again. I want to restore your virtuousness.

Your body is a temple not to be conjoined with emotional or sexual pleasure before marriage.

This is adultery against Me.

*A man that finds a wife finds a good thing*

Proverb 18:22 ESV

So rest in My arms and learn to be My faithful wife. Marriage, I say, is honorable and because of that

*I want to create in you a clean heart and renew a loyal spirit.*

Psalm 51:10 ESV

...within you and present you as an honorable wife.

You are royalty,

Love

My Queen, who deserves a King.

Just fix your gaze on me

because I am the right place to find love,

because I am love and peace.

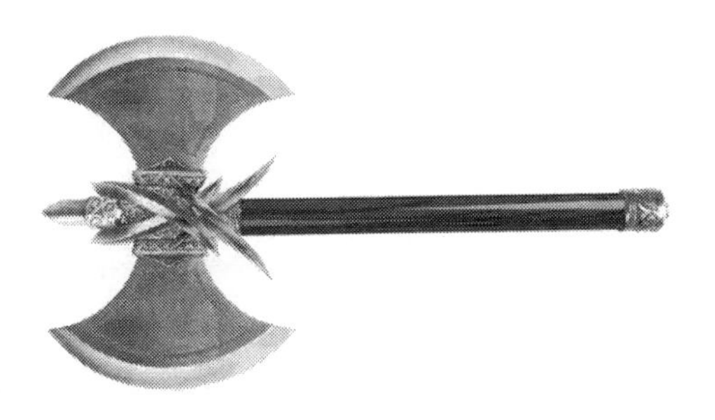

# Battle Axe 12

## Fearfully And Wonderfully Made

**Proverb 18:22 (HCSB)** ***My frame was not hidden from you when I was made in the secret place, when I was woven together in the depths of the earth.***

***Your eyes saw my unformed body; all the days ordained for me were written in your book before one of them came to be.***

## FEARFULLY AND WONDERFULLY MADE

Look up young women,

Look up young men.

There is life ahead of you.

You were not left out of the plans of God. God says,

*For I know the plans I have toward you, Thoughts of peace and NOT EVIL TO GIVE YOU A FUTURE AND HOPE.*

Jeremiah 29:11 ESV

Love isn't between your legs; sexually interlocking and making unlawful covenant on your bed.

Comparing who you are and your features to the next,

That only brings you down.

That's why we gotta love ourselves inside, out and all around.

If you are chocolate, red purple or pale,

You are still beautiful in the sight of the Lord, who created things to be perfect on a ten scale.

Big lip's, no hips, crooked or gapped teeth; God created us in His divine beauty.

For God is the potter and we are His clay; thank You Jesus!

We are fearfully and wonderfully made.

Thank You Jesus! I am fearfully and wonderfully made.

Do you have a small chest and desire big breast? Girl, put your $10,000 dollars back in your pockets. You don't need implants.

Skinny waist, chubby or long face, straight, kinky hair…

God doesn't do favoritism, so therefore we are created equally and fair.

Marvelous are Your works, bestowed in splendor and greatness.

For God formed our inward parts, our frame was not hidden from us when we were made in secret.

*God's eye saw our substance yet unformed.*

Psalm 139:15-16 ESV

God, You are the potter and we are Your clay.

Thank You Jesus! I am fearfully and wonderfully made.

Thank you Jesus! I am fearfully and wonderfully made.

I am fearfully and wonderfully made.

God created us with purpose and destiny.

Not to get distracted with the cares of this world, but to honor Him with our bodies.

God has 20/20 vision; He established the world by His might and wisdom.

He is the maker of all things. He took the dust and water, mixed it into mud, formed it into clay and said, "I want Adam and Eve to look this way."

Thank you Jesus!

I am fearfully and wonderfully made.

*How precious are your thoughts to us O God? How great is the sum of them. If we should count them it would be more in number than the sand*

Psalms 139:17-18 ESV

If we can see ourselves how You see us, O' God, then we would have thoughts of greatness and not negativity.

Eyes that see life and not death, peace and not stress,

There is no need for self hatred, envy, low self esteem, mutilation of the body and suicidal thoughts because You don't believe you're pretty.

Put jealousy on the shelf and blow negativity off of your shoulder and say, "Beauty is in the eye of the beholder."

God, I ask that people will be able to except themselves for who they are, short comings and flaws.

I pray that they can look in the mirror with confidence and hope, be amazed and say, "Thank You Jesus! I am fearfully and wonderfully made!"

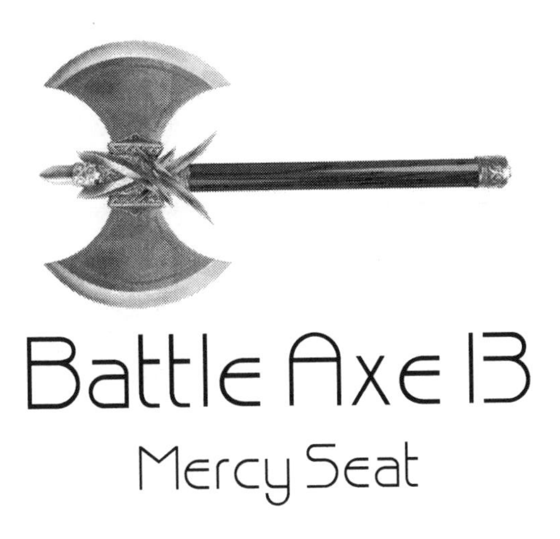

# Battle Axe 13
## Mercy Seat

**Hebrew 2:16-18 (NKJV)** ***For indeed He does not give aid to angels, but He does give aid to the seed of Abraham. Therefore, in all things He had to be made like His brethren, that He might be a merciful and faithful High Priest in things pertaining to God, to make propitiation for the sins of the people. For in that He Himself has suffered, being tempted, He is able to aid those who are tempted.***

## THE MERCY SEAT

Jesus, You took my punishment of death and gave me life.

You rescued me from darkness, now I walk in the light.

For three long vicious hours you were beat, Your blood cried out for me.

Because Your blood covers me, I can now approach the mercy seat.

God, You gave me freedom when I deserved the death penalty.

You forgave my iniquities,

You redeemed my life from the pit,

Oh Lord, how can I forget Your benefits?

When I was locked up in my mind, You gave me the mercy keys.

You became propitiation for the sins of man.

*Jesus You became Human so that YOU might be merciful and faithful high priest in things pertaining to God.*

Hebrews 2:16-18 NSAB

You were tempted and agonized greatly.

As I approach the lid of the Ark, Your mercy seat, I beat my chest and say, "Have mercy on me, a sinner. For you know I am nothing but dust. My days are like grass."

God, You are a judge that judges fairly and righteously.

Eleemon, the most Merciful God.

You are merciful and gracious; slow to anger, abounding in love.

You do not treat me as my sins deserve or repay me according to my iniquities.

*As far as the east is from the west, YOU removed my transgressions from me.*

Psalms 103:8, 12 NIV

Since I know how much you forgave me, I can no longer point my finger condemning others self- righteously, by putting a blind eye to my own sin.

Lord, teach me humility, so I can deal with others kindly.

*For judgment is without mercy to the ones who has shown no mercy*

James 2:13 ESV

As pain from my past confronts me, I will let my heart be a mercy seat that hands out the life sentence of forgiveness.

When I wanted to give up Mercy said No! I will help you embody yourself into their skin so that you can walk in their shoes emotionally.

Lord, infect me with grace that causes an eternal bleeding of mercy when my emotions are insulted daily.

I want to be so sick with Your love that I not seek revenge for any injustices. Let the symptoms of compassion over take me, while I suffer for my loved ones to be set free.

The closer I get to You God; Your mercy will become a virtue that exudes out of my character. The aroma of compassion and kindness will fill the noses of many.

God You are a judge that judges fairly.

YOU God are the Eleemon, the most Merciful God. You are compassionate and gracious; slow to anger, abounding in love.

You will not always accuse, nor will You harbor Your anger forever. YOU do not treat us as our sins deserve or repay us according to our iniquities.

*For as high as the heavens are above the earth so great is YOUR love for those who fear YOU as far as the east is from the west, YOU removed our transgressions from us. YOUR mercy is everlasting to everlasting.*

Psalm 103:9-10 NIV

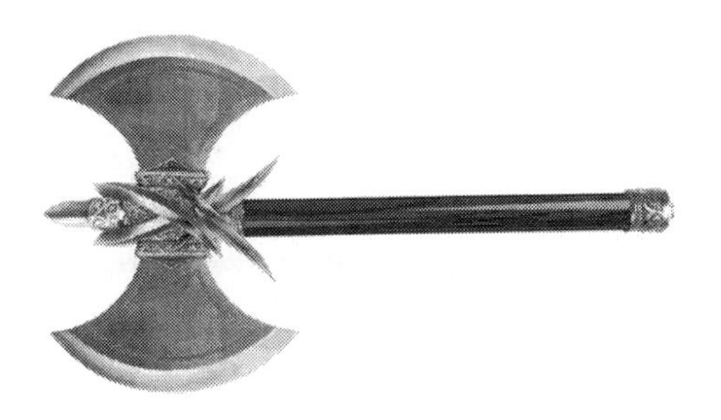

# Battle Axe 14

## God Chosen Woman

**Jeremiah 1:5 (NLT)** ***"I knew you before I formed you in your mother's womb. Before you were born I set you apart and appointed you as my prophet to the nations."***

## WHO IS GOD'S CHOSEN WOMAN?

God says: *you have captured my heart, my treasure, my bride. You hold it hostage with one glance from your eyes like a single jewel on a necklace. Your love delights me, my treasure, and my bride. You are beautiful; my darling beautiful beyond words*

Song of Songs 4:9-10 NLT

I am your royal husband that delights in your beauty.

The inner beautification of your being has been orchestrated by My word.

*I knew you before I formed you in your mother womb; before you were born I set you apart and appointed you as my prophet to the nations*

Jeremiah 1:5 NLT

I have given you children from different nations that you have not met yet.

For I have anointed you for a time such as this, to be a mother figure to nations; leading my daughters and sons to Zion.

Enlarge your house by building additions. Spread out your home, for you will be bursting at the seams.

Your descendants will occupy other nations and resettle the ruin cities (Isaiah 54:1-2 NLT).

Who is God's Chosen Woman?

For her creator is her husband. She is the apple of His eye. She is His faithful servant.

They are one in spirit; for He trusts her with his deepest secrets.

She is a wailing woman woven in intercessory prayer.

The words she speaks are like honey to the bones.

Her gentle words are a tree of life.

She is vitamins to her husband and children's bodies.

Her fruitful words are purifying to the stranger's ear.

Her Godly character is like cinnamon apples to God's nostrils.

This woman thirsts to be intertwined in His presence.

She is God's woman; God;s Chosen Woman for her creator is her husband two becoming one in Spirit.

God's Woman, she is his delight, for her soul thirst after righteousness.

Jesus is her water in every dry season.

He is her bread when she is hungry.

The thorn in her flesh brings her closer to God.

She is consistent even when the ropes of death tried entangling her; floods of destruction tried sweeping over her.

When the grave tried wrapping its rope around her; death laid a trap in her path, but in her distress she cried out to the Lord.

He heard her from His sanctuary. Her cry to Him reached His ears.

JEHOVAH NISSI in victory! She rises and shouts, "Death, where is your sting?"

JEHOVA RAPHA - God who heals all diseases. I know Him intimately to be true, loving Him from the inside out.

My lover is mine and I am His.

For my creator is my husband. The Lord of Heaven armies is His name.

JEHOVA ADONAI my LORD, my MASTER, for You show me where to walk. I give myself to You.

Let Your gracious Spirit continue to lead me forward on a firm footing.

For the glory of Your name O LORD, You have preserved my life. Because of your faithfulness, You have brought me out.

Behold, I am a new creation in You.

Who is God's Chosen woman?

This woman is You!

This woman is We!

This woman is ME!

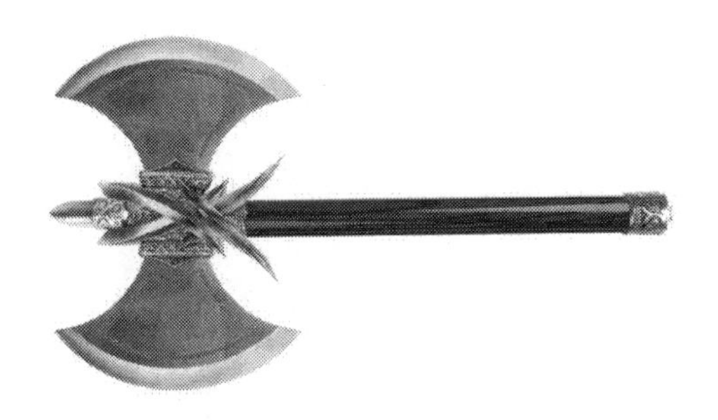

# Battle Axe 15

## God Your Power

**2 Timothy 1:7 (ESV)** ***for God gave us a spirit not of fear but of power and love and self-control.***

## GOD YOUR POWER

When I am feeling like the world is shut down and I don't know what to do, I take my faith I have and count on You.

Because it is You I trust. I let Your love over power my pain when times are tough. Your power and my faith give me the strength to believe spiritually.

Without Your footsteps that shadow my walk way, I am lost and astray.

I can no longer blame my temptation atmosphere on the devil.

I have read the Bible.

My head is on a measurable level.

I realize my relationship with Jesus is not a game to be played.

I am fighting through a world of hell, but with God on my side, I excel.

Some of the people in the world are locked in jail, but those who ask for forgiveness will receive bail.

Your power is indescribable. That's why people have to live life right because on judgment day, they're accountable for their actions.

*May the God of hope fill me with all joy and peace in believing, so that by the power of the Holy Spirit I may abound in hope.*

Romans 15:13 ESV

Your power God, gives off the fragrance of life.

Your powerful scent smells like a garden of flowers.

Jesus your power is like the twin towers; The Most High.

God, Your power is stronger than earthquakes, hurricanes, and snow storms.

Your power is our protection.

*Your right hand, O LORD, glorious in power, your right hand, O LORD, shatters the enemy.*

Exodus 15:6 ESV

Your royal children are hidden in your cloak.

You are a fortress that protects us from the storm.

Mighty Women and Men of valor, believe in the power of the Lord because He believes in the power He invested in you.

God has given us a spirit not of fear, but of power and love and self-control. (2Timothy 1:7 ESV)

Because of Your Power Jesus, to conqueror the grave, I can wipe my tears away with Your mercy.

I have Your DNA. I know You will lead my life on solid ground.

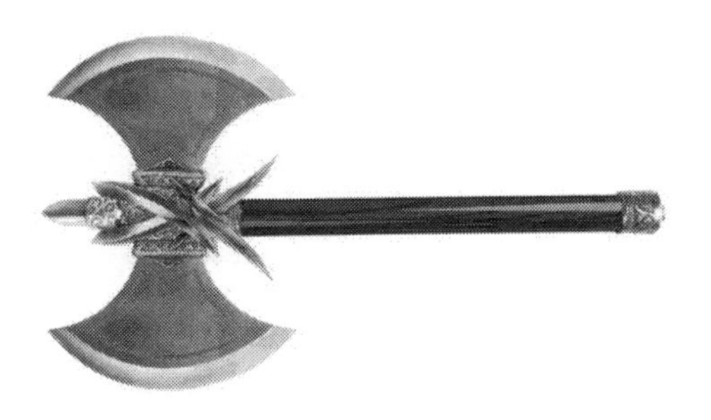

# Battle Axe 16

## Dancing With My Father

**Psalms 30:11 (NSAB)** ***You have turned for me my mourning into dancing;***

***You have loosed my sackcloth and girded me with gladness,***

## DANCING WITH MY FATHER

The angels of Heaven escort me to the dance floor and I see my father in His kingly attire.

The banquet hall floor is filled with the rose petals of forgiveness. The walls are trimmed with 24 karat gold.

I am in awe as His purifying eyes stare at me deeply.

As He gets up off his throne, He walks down the stairs and takes my hand gently and says, “My daughter, you are everything to Me."

Before the world began you were on my mind.

*The king is forever enthralled with Your beauty.*

Psalm 45:11 NIV

My dress is adorned with precious jewels of sapphire and crystal. It was made in heaven, with the essence of Your love.

On the dance floor it’s just You and I. We dance in synch, as the angel sings sweet melodies.

Your hands of mercy are wrapped around my waist.

Your feet of grace guide me across the dance floor.

*In your hands I commit my spirit.*

Psalm 31:5 NIV

*I want to stay tightly connected to you like a tree planted by the stream of water.*

Psalms 1:3 NIV

Your eyes of fire glance at me and You tell me softly again, "The King is in awe of your beauty."

Engrossed in Your glory I dance my problems away.

No longer am I entangled into the cares of this world. I'm focused on You.

I am now entangled in Your presence of peace.

I am a princess dancing with my Father, who is King. My hands are wrapped around Your waist of justification; my head gently lying on Your chest of healing.

I listen to Your heart beat quietly. I can smell the heat of Your breath that smells like cinnamon.

Daddy, breathe on me with Your restoration. Let Your breath feel like rain.

Let Your breath feel like water that waters our seed of destiny.

I am in awe that You would come off of Your throne to dance with me.

We sway side to side.

He twirls me high in the air with one arm, lifting me out the depth of discouragement.

You show me that You are a strong fortress; a refuge in a time of need.

I dance!

I dance!

I dance the night away physically, mentally, emotionally, and spiritually for eternity.

I let my life be a dance floor that I worship on.

I will do the dance move of obedience and faithfulness.

I'll do the dance move of joy as I celebrate you being my Father I adore.

I lay my head in Your bosom and say, "Father, I trust You to guide me."

You have turned my mourning into dancing (Psalms 30:11 NIV).

Oh, I just love dancing with my Father.

*You turned my wailing into dancing; you removed my sackcloth and clothed me with joy, that my heart may sing your praises and not be silent.*

*Lord my God, I will praise you forever.*

Psalms 30:11 – 12 NIV

# Liberation

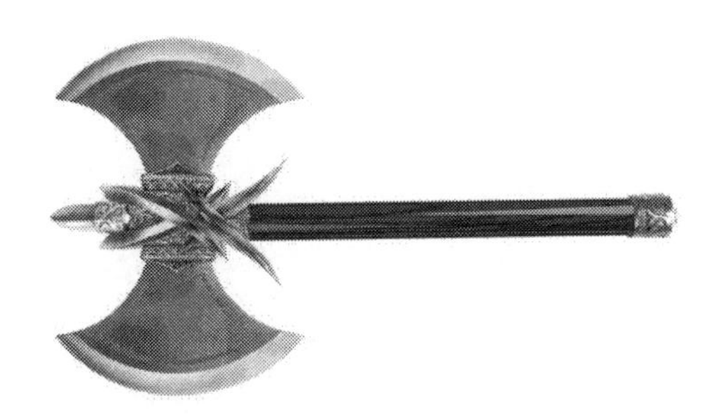

# Battle Axe 17

## I Declare War With My Praise

**Isaiah 61:2-3 (NIV)** ***to proclaim the year of the Lords favor and the day of vengeance of our God, to comfort all who mourn, and provide for those who grieve in Zion to bestow on them a crown of beauty instead of ashes, the oil of gladness instead of mourning and a garment of praise instead of a spirit of heaviness.***

## I DECLARE WAR WITH MY PRAISE

I will use my praise as a weapon to war against the stronghold of my mind.

Satan, I hear you loud and clear combating the voice of God. Yes, in the past I submitted to your voice that toiled with my mind.

I walked in inconsistency; rejecting God because I felt rejected by man. Never should I have put man and God on the same level.

I say I love God, but I do the opposite of what He tells me. These actions make me like the antichrist.

Anti means to go against.

I cannot be married to Jesus and cheating on Him with Satan.

This is the true meaning of inconsistency. Inconsistency gives birth to double mindedness.

His word says *to proclaim the year of the Lords favor and the day of vengeance of our God, to comfort all who mourn, and provide for those who grieve in Zion to bestow on them a crown of beauty instead of ashes, the oil of gladness instead of mourning and a garment of praise instead of a spirit of heaviness.*

Isaiah 61:2-3 NIV

God is saying, "I understand that you feel rejected and left out, but just put on the garment of praise." He says, "I understand why you feel confuse and bewildered, but just put on the garment of praise. I understand what you're going through financially, but just trust Me with this article of clothing, which is praise.

I understand you're having suicidal thoughts, but when you wear the garment of praise it magnifies who I am.

*Now the Lord is the Spirit, and where the Spirit of the Lord is, there is freedom. And we, who with unveiled face all reflect the Lords glory, are being transformed into his likeness with ever-increasing glory, which comes from the Lord, who is the Spirit.*

2 Corinthians 3:17-18 NIV

Your feelings are real, but I am a spirit and need My sons and daughters to elevate their praise, faith, and worship to reach where I am.

You have to press through your flesh and move out of routine. Press through the pain that others have caused or those things you have brought upon yourself.

Press through the pain of feeling like a failure and inadequate in the Kingdom of God.

Let your praise go beyond the veil.

My son, my daughter, let Me mold your mind to wholeness; let Me transform your thinking of who I am.

I am not your abusive father. I am not your abusive mother. I am not the man or woman who manipulated you for selfish gain.

I am not he or she who sexually abused you, but I am He that shall restore.

I am the compassionate Father.

I am the faithful Husband; always pursuing the affections of my wife, the bride of Christ.

No weapon formed against my bride shall prosper. Vengeance is mine and victory is yours. It's time to declare war with your praise.

*Comeback to your first love, if you will return, O Israel return to me," If you put your detestable idols, pride, fear, selfishness, self pity out of my sight and no longer go astray, and if in a truthful, just and righteous way you swear, As surely as the Lord lives, then nations will be blessed by him and in him they will glory.*

Jeremiah 4:1-4 NIV

I declare war with my praise!

I am not going back, but I am looking ahead and declaring that I am everything God has called me to be. But whatever was to my profit, I now consider loss for the sake of Christ.

*What is more, I consider everything a loss compared to the surpassing knowledge of knowing Christ Jesus my Lord, for whose sake I have lost all things, I consider them rubbish that I may gain Christ and be found in him, not having a righteousness of my own that comes from the law religious spirit, but that which is through faith in Christ the righteousness that comes from God and is by faith.*

*I want to know Christ and the Power of his resurrection and the fellowship of sharing in his sufferings, becoming like him in his death and so somehow, to attain to the resurrection from the dead.*

Philippians 3:7-11 NIV

I declare war with my praise, as I put on the full armor of God. Out of my mouth comes my weapon of praise.

It is so easy for me to blame the decisions I have made on the devil, so that I do not have to take responsibility for my actions.

I say this because, Jesus says:

*I have given you authority to trample on snakes and scorpions and to overcome all the power of the enemy; nothing will harm you.*

Luke 10:19 NIV

*Submit yourselves, then to God and he will come near to you, Resist the Devil and he will flee from you. Come near to God and he will come near to you.*

James 4:7-8 NIV

I declare war with my praise because my praise and worship draw me closer to God and the enemy has to flee.

Lord, I ask for forgiveness for not using my authority to please thee. I now declare War with my praise.

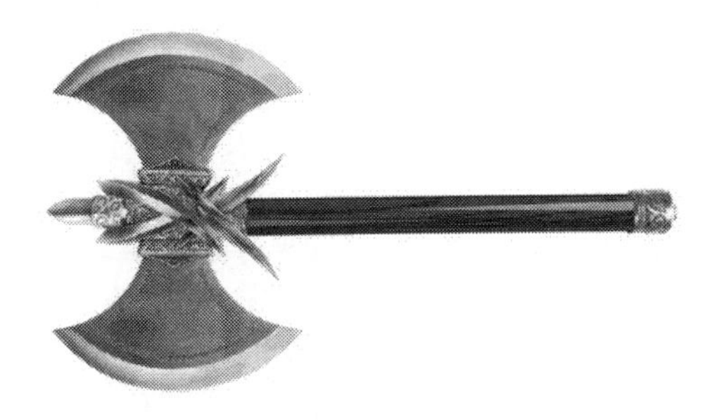

# Battle Axe 18

## I Dare You To Move

**1 Peter 4:10 (NLT)** ***God has given each of you a spiritual gift from His variety of spiritual gifts. Use them well to serve one another.***

## I DARE YOU TO MOVE

God has given each of you a spiritual gift from His variety of spiritual gifts. Use them well to serve one another.

*Do you have the gift of speaking? Then speak as though God himself is here speaking through you. Do you have the gift of helping others? Do it with all the strength and energy that God supplies. Then everything you do will bring glory to God through Jesus Christ. All Glory and power belongs to him forever.*

1 Peter 4:11 NLT

*Perfect love casts out all fear*

1 John 4:18 NLT

I dare you to move into the things God has for you.

Be wise men and let the oil in your heart continue to burn. We don't know when the bridegroom is coming.

I dare you to move in your God given talents to build up the Kingdom.

Let's not slack spiritually on the gifts God has entrusted us with.

*Be the faithful servant, who invested his five bags of silver and made double, the Lord said good and faithful servant you have been faithful over a few things come and I will make you a ruler over many*

Mathew 25:21 NKJV

I dare you to move! Let's be ready to answer the call and always be alert.

It's time to come out of your spiritual coma. God, I ask that you send restoration and revitalize the body of Christ from dead bones of sickness and repetition.

God, break down church tradition. It's time out for church play; let's worship You radically.

I dare you to move fully into trusting God and His promises.

I dare you to move in your faith.

I dare you to move out of your self-centered ways.

Let's began to drink from the cup of love because that's real servant hood. Looking through the eyes of Christ we realize we have to die to the flesh in order to have life.

I dare you to move and go deeper into the word of God! Be spiritually fit and challenge your mind. Be willing to be stretched by the hands of God.

I dare you to move into transformation; stepping out of your old ways of life and into the new.

Let go of the hurt and un-forgiveness of broken relationships. God, open the hearts of your people.

Lost sheep come back! God has not forgotten about you; let Jesus take control of your life.

Prodigal girl, boy, man or women… your Father in heaven has been graciously waiting on your return.

I dare you to tell the devil that he is no longer in control.

I dare you to run back to the King of Kings, the Lord of Lords, and the Almighty.

The chain of wickedness has been broken, destroyed, and annihilated with the blood of Christ.

Lost sheep that are in and out of the church, Jesus says, "I tell you the truth, if you had faith as small as a mustard seed you could say to this mountain move from here to there and it would move nothing would be impossible." (Matthew 17:20 NIV)

Church I dare you to move on faith alone, with God given strength.

It's time to move the obstacles of life out of our way so that we can truly step into the things of God.

I dare you to move even if you're the only one.

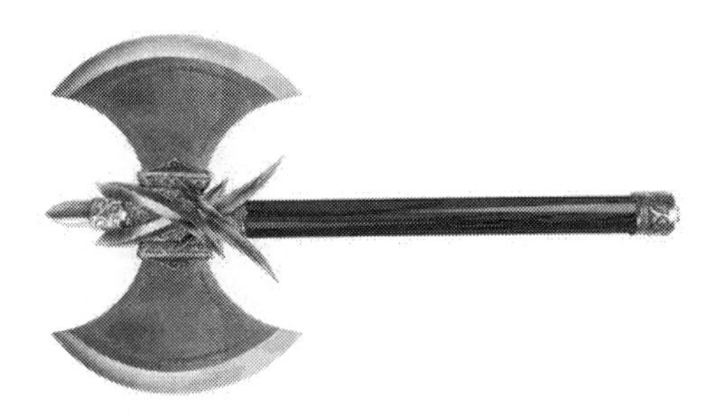

# Battle Axe 19

## Meditation Of Galatians 1:10

**Galatians 1:10 (ESV)** ***For am I now seeking the approval of man, or of God? Or am I trying to please man? If I were still trying to please man, I would not be a servant of Christ.***

## THE MEDITATION OF GALATIANS 1:10

*For do I now persuade men or God? Do I seek to please Men? For If I yet please men, I should not be the servant of Christ*

Galatian 1:10 ESV

Why do I seek to please men?

The reason is because I look for opportunity to show off, to gain approval.

I hunt for recognition, look for compliments and search for significance… I try to find who I am through other people's opinions.

I aim to be immortal in the heart of man; never will they forget who I am.

I please man because I don't want to be rejected.

My no, in my heart, becomes a yes.

My interior motives are for selfish gain.

I tell you what you want to hear only to self promote my so call "godly" agendas.

I bow down to the spirit of compromising, to so call make peace and not be argumentative, even if this means agreeing with Satan on his territory.

Why do I lie? Sadly, to please man...

I fear because my confidence has been in what people thought of me.

I realize I have fallen in the trap of approval addiction and idolizing people.

God, I realize I cannot call myself a servant and please man.

God, I have been rebellious by choosing man over You.

I have looked at You as if You were my equal.

Everyday Your light has caught me red handed, in both my heart and action.

In this walk, God, I realize I have to lose my reputation.

Lord, search my heart and show me who I really am underneath every spiritual conversation. God, show me my hearts motives.

I can persuade men to follow Christ but I don't have to please men to follow Christ.

This is the meditation of Galatians 1:10

God, I ask that Your blood bind up this people pleasing spirit.

God, I ask that You break the generational curse of this spirit.

Lord Jesus, let Your Holy boldness saturate our hearts so that I would be a God pleaser in my motives and conversation.

*Where the spirit of the Lord is there is liberty*

2 Corinthians 3:17 NKJV

*The blind receive their sight, and the lame walk, the lepers are cleansed, and the deaf hear, the dead are raised up, and the poor have the gospel preached to them.*

*And blessed is he, whosoever shall not be offended in me.*

Matthew 11:5-6 KJV

Christ, I realize that when I strive to please people, in reality I am saying with unspoken words that I am offended by what you stand for.

*Whatever you do, work at it with all your heart as working for the Lord, not for men.*

Colossians 3:23 NIV

This is the Meditation of Galatians 1:10

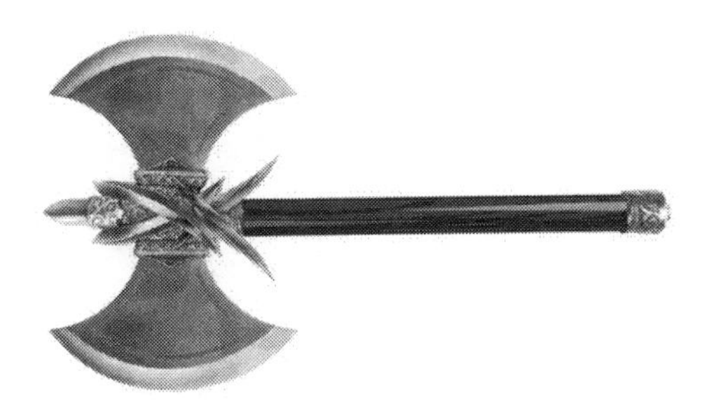

# Battle Axe 20

## Liberate The Father

**1Peter 4:8 (NIV)** ***Above all, love each other deeply, because love covers over a multitude of sins.***

## LIBERATE THE FATHER

God, I see why You say not to put Your trust in man. Man has too many fallacies and imperfections for one's heart to handle.

Could you still love someone if God revealed to you who they truly were?

Would you treat them differently if they walked deliberately in sin and then preached behind the pulpit, shared the gospel, visited the sick, or laid hands on you?

Could you love them unconditionally?

Ask yourself, do you really love your neighbor as yourself?

Do you love them because they haven't done anything to hurt you?

Do you love them because of what they do?

Ask, why do you love?

Is your love conditional, or do you love that person with your mouth, but your heart is far from them?

Could you love that person if they raped you physically or emotionally?

Could you love them if they continued to lie and all you are left with is another broken promise?

Could you love this person if you have seen this person abuse your mom and your family and have felt their abuse yourself?

Who is this person you love and hate to love?

Could this person be the father that you have not liberated?

He stands behind the bars of your spirit, while serving a life sentence for un-forgiveness. When are you willing to give yourself parole and set him free?

When will you allow forgiveness to set you free?

Where is your willing heart of forgiveness?

Your hurtful words explode like an aneurism; eyes blood shot red, face cringing in reaction to a distorted mind. You fight back tears and your body becomes numb, as the cycle of mental abuse continues. The cycle of meeting men who nurture the little girl inside you repeats itself. Sadly, it only hurts her over and over again.

Your hurt has become your shades, blocking you from the Son, Jesus the Christ. He is the only one who reveals soothing truth to your oozing wounds.

The bowels of your emotions have blasted like an atomic bomb inside your stomach, disturbing the atmosphere in which you stand. With a heavy cramp you bend down on your knees crying out, "God take me to the root of my issue."

Why am I running from man to man?

Why am I so needy for love and attention?

Why am I so codependent?

Lord, my addictions to sex, drug and alcohol only make me feel so empty. This hole in my heart can't continue to be filled by lies. This is why I seek truth.

Truth is the seed that needs to be planted in the soil of my mind. Truth is the nutrient that helps my faith grow.

Truth is the battle axe to the flesh. God, I want to be connected to Your Truth.

Without Your Truth, I am a half-dead body choking on the blood of life; dead to sin and alive in Christ.

Without truth I am nothing but dead bones. God, be the Gardner of my spirit. God, I'm ready to deal with my past, present and future issues. Not by my might but by walking in the truth.

*Jesus says I am the way and the truth and the life. No one comes to the Father except through me.*

John 14:6 NIV

*I am the true vine, and my Father is the gardener. He cuts off every branch in me that bears no fruit, while every branch that does not bear fruit he prunes so that it will be even more fruitful*

John 15:1-5 NIV

I give up trying to be my own God. I'm done letting the devil father my issues with lies.

My daughter, I hear your cry and this cry is loosening your numbness, so that you can feel again. I have weakened your muscles so that you have no energy to fight back tears.

Let your cry spring out like an ocean wave. I had to bring you to this point so you can hear my sweet whispers. I am not mad at you daughter. I just know the path you were taken was a dead end. My children, I love, I chastise. I am He that gives the divine pruning. To see me as your Father you have to set your biological father free. Liberate him, so that you can be free from the bondage of sin and cycles.

Drop your rights to rage, anger, frustration, and rejection. Dismiss this case you have against your father. Let him be delivered from the prison bars of your spirit. In My hand I hold freedom keys. I will unleash you and let you keep these keys to unleash your father. Liberate! Liberate! Liberate your father and be set free.

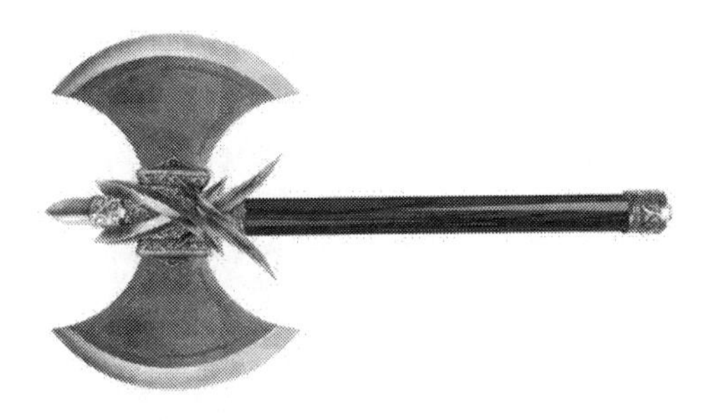

# Battle Axe 21

## Liberty

**Mathew 11:28-30 (NLT)** ***Then Jesus said, "Come to me, all of you who are weary and carry heavy burdens, and I will give you rest. Take my yoke upon you. Let me teach you, because I am humble and gentle at heart, and you will find rest for your souls. For my yoke is easy to bear, and the burden I give you is light."***

# LIBERTY

*For I was hungry and you gave me something to eat, I was thirsty and you gave me something to drink, I was a stranger and you invited me in.*

Mathew 25:35 NIV

You, or a loved one might have AIDS/HIV, but God's Healing is not in vain.

He says I am Jehovah Rapha; Your healer of your sickly being.

*If my people would are called by my name turn from their wicked ways I will hear them from heaven and will forgive them from their sins and restore their land My eyes will be open and my ears attentive to every prayer made in this place*

*2Chronicles 7:14-16 ESV*

*Do not judge others, and you will not be judged for you will be treated as you treat others. The standard you use in judging is the standard by which you will be judged*

Mathew 7:1-2 NLT

See Lord, this judgmental and hypocritical spirit has caused hurting people to suffer in silence with a deadly disease called HIV.

For my people perish for lack of knowledge from walking in liberty of knowing one's status.

People in church who are walking in the flesh and portraying to be an angel of light have become a stumbling block to the wounded soul. This has caused this soul to reject the church as a whole.

These stones of sickly emotions have built a monument of rejection, isolation, fear, depression, abandonment, loneliness, guilt, grief, and discrimination.

Your incarcerated pain has caused you to be physically and spiritually drained.

These stones have caused you to see out the eyes of pain; neglecting to see the ax in Jesus' hand that yearns to dismantle these stones with His unconditional love that says:

*Come to me all of you who are weary and carry heavy burdens and I will give you rest, take my yoke upon you. Let me teach you because I am humble and gently at heart and you will find rest for your souls. For my yoke is easy and my burden is light.*

Mathew 11:28-29 NLT

Let me take that heart of stone and give you a heart of flesh.

*I hear your heart that says" You know what I long for, Lord; you hear my every sigh.*

*My heart beats wildly, my strength fails and I am going blind my loved ones and friends stay away fearing my disease. Even my own family stands at a distance"*

Psalm 38:9-11 NLT

Although people reject you because your family and loved ones are suffering with AIDS/HIV, know this:

*The Lord your God will not reject his people; he will not abandon his special possession.*

Psalm 94:14 NLT

He who knew no sin, became sin, so that you can become the righteousness of God.

This is an invitation to the sexually promiscuous man or woman. God wants to fill your void of emptiness.

To the men or women who have aids or know someone with this disease, here's an invitation to stand in the gap.

*The good news is Jesus was despised and rejected by men; he was wounded for our transgressions; he was crushed for our iniquities; upon him was the punishment that brought us peace, and by his stripes we are healed.*

*All like sheep have gone astray; we have turned—every one—to his own way; and the LORD has laid on him the iniquity of us all.*

*He was oppressed, and he was afflicted, yet he opened not his mouth; he had done no violence, and there was no deceit in his mouth.*

*Yet it was the will of the LORD to crush him; the transgressors; yet he bore the sin of many, and makes intercession for the transgressors*

Isaiah 53:7-10 NLT

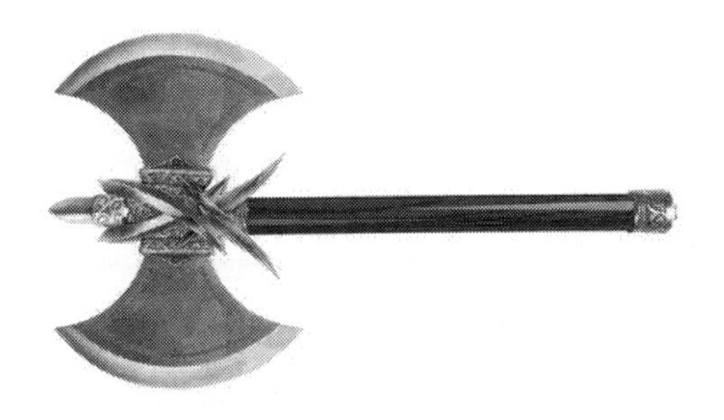

# Battle Axe 22

## Prepare Me A Body

**Ephesians 6:11-18 (NIV)** ***I put on the armor of God, the breast plate of righteousness, the helmet of salvation, the belt of truth around my waist and with your feet fitted with the readiness that comes from the Gospel of Peace. Also the shield of faith, and the sword of the spirit which is the word of God.***

## GOD PREPARE ME A BODY

God, I want to be created in your splendid image.

*Bestow on me the crown of beauty instead of ashes. Instead of mourning I want the garment of praise. Instead of a spirit of despair, anoint me with the oil of gladness. God use me to renew the ruined cities that have been devastated for generations*

Isaiah 61:3-4 NIV

God, prepare me a body so that I can do Your will. The field of crop is dying.

God, prepare me a body.

I want to be the farmer who sows the seed of Your word that gives everlasting life.

Satan, you are a lie straight from the pits of hell.

You have no power to uproot the living word of God.

God, prepare me a body splendid in Your image.

God, fill me with Your Holy Ghost, so that I may walk in Your ways.

God, prepare me as I put on the armor of God, which consist of the breast plate of righteousness, the helmet of salvation, the belt of truth around my waist and with your feet fitted with the readiness that comes from the Gospel of Peace. Also, prepare me to put on the Shield of Faith and the Sword of the Spirit, which is the word of God. God, it is this preparation that will bring me eternal strength.

God, prepare me a body so that I may walk in Your way. Tear down the temple that I have created with my bare hands. God, reconstruct my temple with Your spirit.

*The foxes have holes and the birds of the air have nest but the son of man has nowhere to rest his head.*

Mathew 8:20 NKJV

God, prepare me a body.

I am crying out for the Son of Man to rest His spirit in me.

Faith without works is dead, so I no longer want to be sitting in the pews, just being a hearer of the word.

I want to be a doer.

God says: *My people come to a preacher as the usually do and sit before him to listen to his words, but they do not put them into practice. With their mouth they express devotion, but their hearts are greedy for unjust gain.*

*Indeed, to them he is nothing more than one who sings love songs with a beautiful voice and plays an instrument well, for they hear the preacher, but do not put them into practice.*

Ezekiel 33:31-32 NIV

I no longer want to sit down on Your word.

I no longer want to come to church for the choir and a spiritual high that erodes away.

I no longer want to come to church with lustful eyes, but God I want to come with a pure heart; desiring to serve You, in spirit and in truth.

I rebuke the spirit of a Pharisees serving my God in hypocrisy.

I tell you my friends, do not be afraid of those who kill the body and after that can do no more.

*Fear him who, after killing of the body has power to throw you into hell.*

Luke 12:4-5 NLT

God, You have given me a choice to repent of all my crooked ways and how I misused Your temple.

So God, have your way inside of me.

Prepare me a body.

*You said the harvest is plentiful the workers are few*

Mathew 9:37 NASB

God, you said ask and it will be given to you, seek and you will find, knock and the door will be open to you. (Mathew 7:7 NIV)

So God, prepare me a body, because I'm dying to do the work of the Lord.

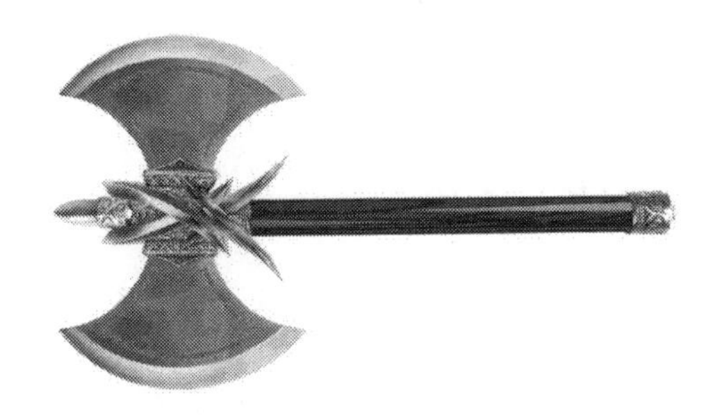

# Battle Axe 23

## The Molested Womb

**Psalm 34:18 (NSAB)** ***The Lord is near to the brokenhearted And saves those who are crushed in spirit.***

## THE MOLESTED WOMB

Does anyone see me?

Does anyone hear me?

Does anyone care?

I am the molested wounds crying out for healing.

In my defiance, I cry out, "Heal me."

In my anger, I cry out.

In my promiscuity I cry rescue me, for I feel dirty and worthless.

Would anybody believe the scars to my story?

I have been physically, emotionally, and sexually tortured.

What you see is an adult, but inside I feel like that 9 year old girl that is screaming for love.

He touched me… He raped me of my man hood… He touched me and she touched me and trampled over my woman hood. My innocence and purity is gone. The touch of anyone brings back painful memories and the recollection of the scared tissues of my womb.

The emotional molested wounds cry RESCUE ME FROM ME!

Suicide is banging on the door shouting, "Let me in!"

I'm one second from letting suicide in because I feel at fault for daddies and mommies divorce and his 10 year prison sentence.

It's my fault!

Uncle,

Aunty,

Cousins,

Brother or sister touched me over, over and over again.

These weird emotions make me confused.

I am an adult now. I could have told him or her to stop.

I am angry because I could not fix my mouth to say no.

I didn't fight back because this is what I knew as love.

These molested wounds are the reason I am entangled in homosexuality.

It's the reason for the need for control,

It's the reason for my insecurity and lack of trust.

I have been taking showers three times a day to erase away the smell.

The foul stench of your cologne and the rotten smell of your perfume make me want to puke.

I hate church because of you.

You were supposed to be my mentor and they call you Deacon.

If they only knew you were the man pretending to wear sheep clothing and turned out to be a wolf.

You were the one who took my manhood.

They call you First Lady! You were supposed to be my spiritual mother, yet you betrayed me for my woman hood.

You introduced me to masturbation; a feeling that replays to your touch.

This feeling plays with my mind and is indirectly molestation of self. This is psychological suicide.

I am an adult, but the wounded child is crying out deliver me… "Give birth to this still born death baby," for it can no longer be intertwined with my spirit.

The placenta of my mind, body, and spirit and soul! I have been in labor half my life.

*The Lord is near to the broken hearted and saves the crushed in spirit.*

Psalm 34:18 NSAB

I will name him Elioenai Hosanna Jada, which means God delivers us. For He knows the pain and He has set me free!

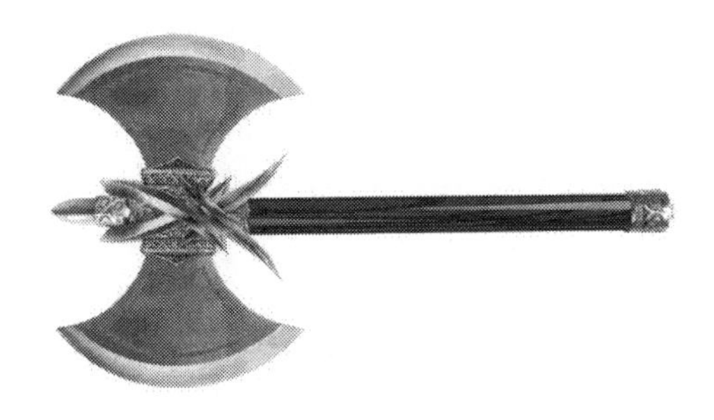

# Battle Axe 24

## Sloth

**Proverb 6:9-11 (NIV)** ***How long will you lie there, you sluggard? When will you get up from your sleep? A little sleep, a little slumber, a little folding of the hands to rest and poverty will come on you like a thief and scarcity like an armed man.***

## SLOTH

Do you just exist or are you living?

Really! Realize that you were made to be a living being that expresses to the world the gift that you are to your community.

So do you just exist or are you living?

This question should provoke you to take a deep self-inventory.

Life's hardships leave you strength-less, debating if life is worth living. Depression has hit your life like a tsunami that leaves you hopeless.

These demons speak to your soul, hounding and begging you for a negative emotional out pour that will leave you slumped over life.

God created you to worship Thee, instead you bow down to the god of procrastination and the god of laziness. Sloth has you walking in circles and climbing mountains but never reaching the top for victory.

You're forever doing, but ain't doing anything to fulfill your God giving purpose in the earth.

You're living a fictionist life: fake identity. Your blinded eyes cannot see the true and living God.

You cannot live life like an unresponsive dead brain person who is hooked up to a ventilator of oxygen. Existing, but not living; breathing but lifeless.

The talents and abilities inside you lay dormant; waiting and crying out to live out a legacy.

God wants you to listen to the sound that says defeat is not the ending to your story.

So do you just exist or are you living?

Your spirit man says I want to be like the ants; small yet wise, with little strength, but storing my food in the summer.

You have been hearing the wrong sound for too long and now you're walking dead bones. Buried underneath your wounds are discovery, potential and security. This is the time, this is the hour, this is the moment, and God says I am calling for the release and the manifestation of the investment that I have placed in you.

*How long will you lie there, you sluggard? When will you get up from your sleep? A little sleep, a little slumber, a little folding of the hands to rest and poverty will come on you like a thief and scarcity like an armed man.*

Proverb 6:9-11 NIV

Oh sluggard spirit, I see you are the constrictor snake that is wrapped around the souls of many. Your strength crushes the rib cage in two. Oh, can these dead bones live again! Yes! Silver and gold I have none, pick up your mat and walk. Walk into your destiny and walk into your deliverance. Scattered bones, I command you to reconnect into the skeletal body that you once were. Replenish thee with flesh. Oh, can these dead bones live again? Yes God, fill me again and renew my mind. In God, I am redefined.

# Peace

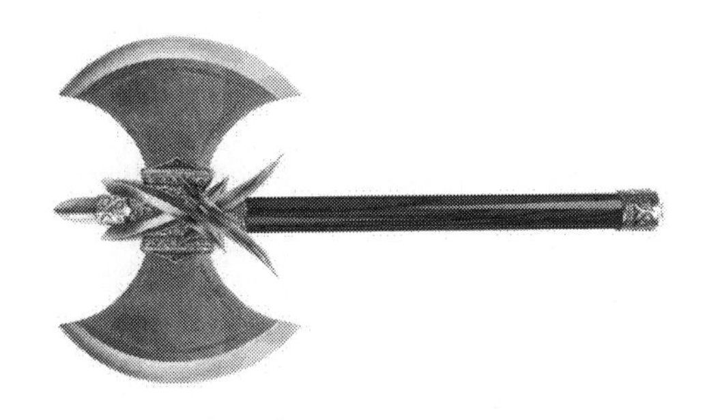

# Battle Axe 25

## Motivation

**Philippians 4:13 (NIV)** ***I can do all things through him who strengthens me.***

## MOTIVATION

Motivate me to become a successful woman in this world today.

When times are tough I know everything will be okay.

I thank You for the good times and bad times in my life. That's why I continue to stay motivated.

The love I have for You will never be betrayed because I know You will have my back any day.

This is why I stay motivated. The goals I have can be achieved, no matter if they are hard to reach.

I can do all things through Him who strengthens me. (Philippians 4:13 NIV)

Whoever said the road to success would be an easy one?

I am a strong woman, handling the struggle under faith you see.

I stay motivated knowing it will keep me civilized and situated.

My flesh continues to stay in combat with my spirit, but because I let You motivate me to do well in life, I ignore it.

As I cry out Jesus, You motivate me to become a strong woman.

Jesus you said, "I am the way, the truth and the life. No one comes to the father except through me." (John 14:6 NLT)

See, because I believe, You motivate me to become anything I want to be.

Jesus, You are my motivator. All my trust, faith and mercy belong to You, my creator.

My heart, mind, body and spirit are secured with Your love.

When I fall, I get back up. Your love for me will not be forsaken, but used for motivation.

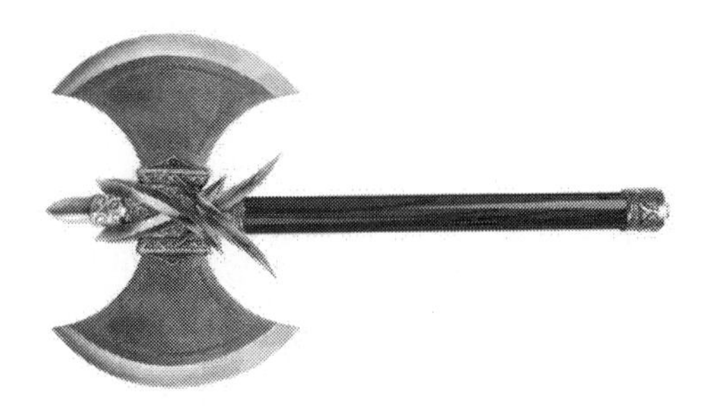

# Battle Axe 26

## I Am The Door

**Psalm 51:7, 10 (NLT)** ***I will give you a clean heart and contrite spirit. I will blot out your sins; I will wash you clean as snow. I will purify you from your guilt; I will renew a loyal spirit in you.***

## I AM THE DOOR

I am the door of the sheep.

I am the door. By Me, if any man enter in, He shall be saved.

So therefore, there is no other way.

*I am the good shepherd; I am He that gives His life for His sheep.*

*Those that sneak in through the back door are a robber and a thief.*

*My sheep hear my voice and I know them and they follow me.*

*My purpose is to give a rich and satisfying life. I am the good shepherd.*

*The good shepherd sacrifices his life for his sheep.*

John 10:1-5 NSAB

I have other sheep too that are not in this sheepfold. Muslim, Buddhist… all those who follow a false hope, I am calling them out.

Harden not your heart when you hear My voice.

I conquered death so that you may be resurrected in Me. I give living water.

Anyone who drinks the water I give will never thirst again.

*I will become a fresh, bubbling spring within you, giving you eternal life.*

John 4:14 NLT

Don't put your confidence in power or people. There is no help for you there.

*When they breathe their last and they return to the grave and all their plans die with them, but joyful are those who have the God of Israel,*

Psalm 146:3-4 NLT

*Who believes that Jesus is the way the truth and the life.*

John 14:6 NLT

*God made heaven and earth, the sea and everything in them.*

ACTS 4:24 NIV

He keeps every promise forever.

He gives Justice to the oppressed and food to the hungry. Let your soul hunger after Me. I will breast feed you spiritual milk until your able to chew meat.

The food I give is nourishment to your mind, body, and spirit.

The Lord frees prisoners who are in sexual bondage.

Are you tied up by suicidal thought, self hatred, fear, impurity, lustful pleasures, idolatry, hostility, jealousy, outbursts of anger, selfishness, envy and people pleasing?

Try Me and I will give you a clean heart and a contrite spirit.

I will blot out your sins; I will wash you clean as snow.

I will purify you from your guilt; I will renew a loyal spirit in you. (Psalm 51:7, 10 NLT)

*I am the great I am! I AM the fruit that produces love, joy, peace, patience, kindness, goodness, fruitfulness, gentleness and self control*

Galatians 5:22-24 NLT

*I am the true grapevine and my Father is the Gardner. He cuts off every branch that does not produce fruit and He prunes the branches that do bear fruit so they will produce even more. Remain in me and I will remain in you. You cannot be fruitful unless you remain in me. Apart from me you can do nothing. If you remain in me and my word in you, you may ask for anything you want and it will be granted.*

John 15:1-7 NIV

I am He that opens the eyes of the blind. I Am He that binds up the broken hearted.

I am close to all who calls on me. Yes, all who call Me in spirit and in truth.

I hear the cries for help and I will rescue you.

I am protection. I am the door; walk through. I chose you, you didn't chose Me.

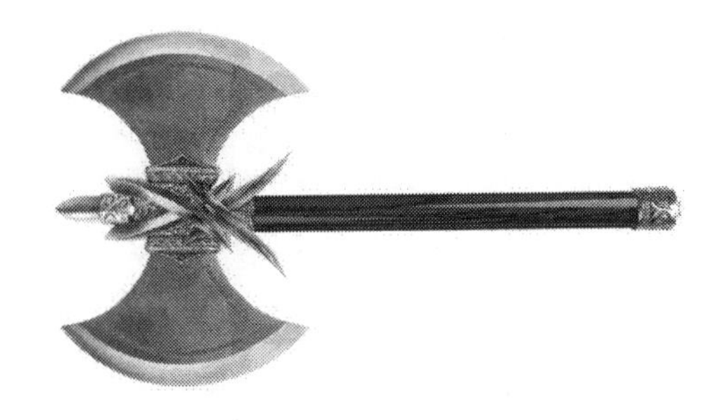

# Battle Axe 27

## God's Grace

**Isaiah 53:3-8 (NIV)** ***Pierced for us sinners crushed for our iniquities. The punishment that brought us peace was wrapped around him and by his wounds we are healed. Oppressed and afflicted, He was led like a lamb to the slaughter. Jesus bared the transgressions of many, making intercession for the transgressors.***

## GOD'S GRACE

Grace is free yet it wasn't cheap and our nation takes God's grace for granted. It's like saying ABC and 1, 2, 3's with an ease.

God's Grace is a battle won because it took purification, sinless and righteousness.

The blood of Jesus…

His Son from the bosom…

His grace and mercy is renewed…

Everyday grace was the price that was paid.

*Jesus took our infirmities and carried our sorrows on the cross. Pierced for us sinners crushed for our iniquities. The punishment that brought us peace was wrapped around him and by his wounds we are healed.*

Isaiah 53:3-5 NSAB

God's Grace, His amazing Grace, trying to work to heaven is a lost race.

*Oppressed and afflicted, He was led like a lamb to the slaughter, yet he silently put love to action*

Isaiah 53:7 NSAB

God, Your grace we appreciate. Your grace is true love that stitches up the wounded soul.

*Jesus bared the transgressions of many, making intercession for the transgressors*

Isaiah 53:8 NSAB

God, Your grace; Jesus Your loving grace is joy to the patched soul.

Devil, you can have death, but God's grace can't be stolen.

I am no longer in captivity and walking on egg shells. I am free, dying to the flesh so true life can intercede through me.

I once was a fake sitting in the church saying, "I accepted, knew and appreciated Your grace."

Tears roll down my eyes. I realized it was I that helped pound the three nails and tear the flesh from the vein. It was I that didn't care and helped brutalize You. But, you screamed, "Father forgive them, for they know not what they do."

You forgave an entire nation.

As I look deeply, I will no longer take Your grace lightly.

The Lord, my strength! My shield!

My heart shall trust in Him.

My redeemer; my joy for Him is like a barren woman. I stand in humbleness as I experience the unfailing love, obedience and compassion Jesus has on me.

My soul stays in line. I trust God because I don't want to be shaken from the true vine.

All I can say is that I will win the race, not by my pace, but because of my relationship that says thanks for Your grace.

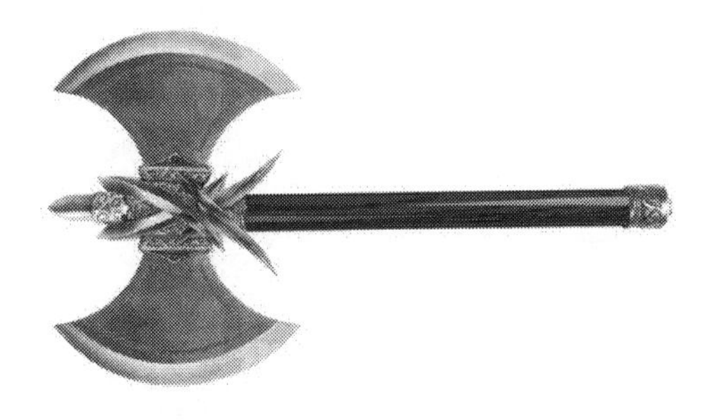

# Battle Axe 28

## The Storm Is Over

**2 Corinthians 4:8-9 (NSAB)** ***We are hard-pressed on every side, yet not crushed; we are perplexed, but not in despair, persecuted but not forsaken; struck down but not destroyed.***

## THE STORM IS OVER

I know you feel the hail and rain splattering on your head harshly.

I know the thunder and lightning is scaring you, but I'm here to tell you the storm is almost over.

This storm has you feeling like a battle you have already lost, but what keeps you going is your knowledge that God is the boss.

You have experienced how flesh can demonize your spirit at a time in your life when your spirit should be overtaking your flesh.

This storm that's in your life symbolizes your spiritual warfare, yet knowing that Jesus is going to get you out will be your fire filled testimony.

This storm has caused loved ones to walk away or not understand your story. But, knowing Jesus is by your side and listening gives you a chance to shout for glory. This storm has shattered you to rock bottom; at a low you have never been, but know this is your testimony.

Yes, the Devil had you under his captivity. He used you until your spirit was sucked almost dry.

Your cry out to Jesus caused Him to cut the chains that your emotionally bruised body was in.

Jesus grabbed your hand softly, but with a grip and said, "The storm is over."

Jesus says, "I am your husband, your best friend, mother and father.

I will never hurt you nor leave your side. I am always here to give you advice and love you because you are mine.

When you are experiencing darkness, I will go beyond it all to deliver the light.

I am the Almighty! I am the one who will give you mercy and pull you out the fire the hell storm.

I will replenish what was lost.

Just listen to the tingling motion in your spirit. That's My voice.

Please don't be rebellious against Me. I will never tell you wrong. You just have to believe!"

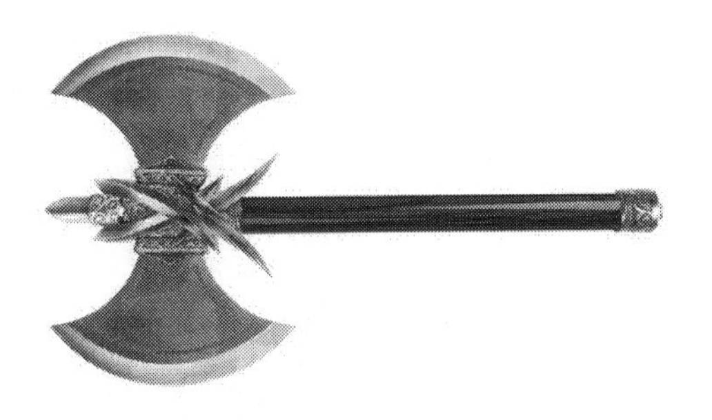

# Battle Axe 29

## The Joy Of The Lord Is My Strength

**Proverb 17:22 (KJV)** ***A merry heart doeth good like medicine.***

## THE JOY OF THE LORD IS MY STRENGTH

So many times God I just wanted to give up and say, "Why me?" I want to complain and look at things selfishly.

But that's not Christ like, so I have to wipe the crud away from my eyes to see that these things are coming, so that my pride can leave and my ego can be crushed.

So When I face another battle concerning my life style, it will willingly scream, "In God only, do I trust! I'm in a warzone and I'm not giving up any ground."

I have been made for this and purpose will be produced, as the Holy Spirit guides me in all truth. When I stop complaining and wistfully looking within, I'll take my losses and quit trying to win with my own strength.

As I look to the cross I see that Jesus died a painful death sacrificially. So the least I can do is to join in His suffering and say no more digging empty wells. God, you are worthy!

We know that this race isn't given to the swift, but to those who endure with strength.

As my flesh is gutted out like a fish, my spirit man screams the joy of the Lord is my fortress.

You God are my CHEDVA; my joy.

I call you CHARA; my calm delight.

Your words are the food I eat generating the nutrients, comfort, and peace sustaining me.

Deep within, my soul has been spiritually infested by the jubilation of the Lord.

The joy of the Lord is my strength, so I am not grieved and I refuse to be depressed.

I count it all in joy when I get these life tests.

I shall not want, I shall not fear because when I feel like God is far away, He is just that near.

He is the wall that I can lean on. He is the strength to my bones.

I serve a mighty God, one I can cast my burdens on.

When things are getting hard my spirit man screams the acronym for J.O.Y.! Jesus Over You Satan!

You cannot steal my joy.

God, Your strength gives me the power to win, conquer and defeat. I serve a God with an infinite winning streak. For this world is only a tent, and I serve a King with many mansions.

Whom do I have in heaven but You? And earth has nothing I desire but You.

I am the star in that dark sky. On top of that hill I am that beacon of light.

My life I live tells a Christ like story, for Him alone shall get the glory.

I've been beat down and drugged in the mud, yet I'm still victorious.

You are my Aleve and Excedrin.

*A merry heart doeth good like medicine.*

Proverb 17:22 KJV

Seeking happiness in God gives birth to joy.

I count my life as a loss to the surpassing knowledge of Christ.

He is my contentment, for I put no confidence in the flesh. As long as I am serving God, I am blessed.

I am blessed and highly favored. You watch over me to perform your word.

I am blessed!

I am from the free seed, the free woman Sarah, who gave birth to promise in Isaac.

The joy of the Lord is my strength. I am blessed!

*Many are the affliction of the righteous, but the LORD delivers him out of them all.*

Psalm 34:19 KJV

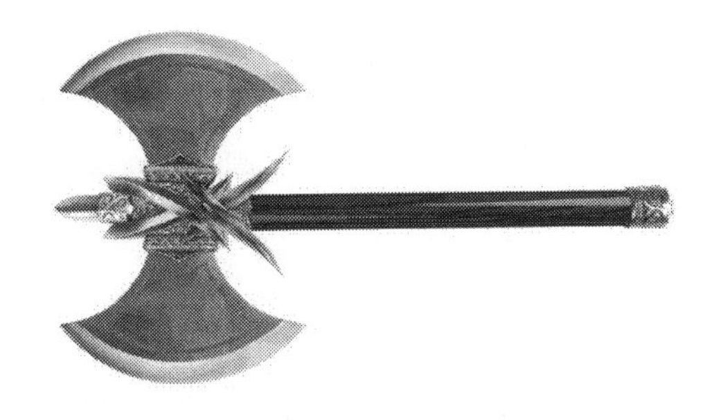

# Battle Axe 30

## Before The Throne

**Isiah 6:1-2 (KJV) The** ***Lord sits on a throne high and lifted up and his train of his robe fills the temple. Above it stood seraphim; each had six wings: with covered his face, with two he covered his feet, two he flew and one cried to another holy, holy, holy is the Lord God almighty the whole earth is filled with your glory.***

## BEFORE THE THRONE

He who sits on the throne has the appearance of jasper and carnelian and around the throne was a rainbow that had the appearance of an emerald, encircled the throne. (Rev.4:3 NKJV )

Hallelujah, you are my God!

From the throne came flashes of lightning, and rumbling and peals of thunder, and before the throne was burning seven torches which are the seven spirits of God Rev 4:6 NKJV

You are JEHOVAH- JIREH; Our provider.

You are JEHOVAH-NISSI; Our Banner.

You are JEHOVAH- SHALOM; Our perfect peace.

You are JEHOVAH-TSID-KENU; Our righteousness.

You are JEHOVAH –SHAMMAH; You are our present help.

You are JEHOVAH SABOATH; The Lord of Host, our protector.

You are JEHOVAH – RAAH; You Lord are our Shepherd. You keep us safe.

You are JEHOVAH RAPHA our Physician and Healer.

You are EL ROI; The God of Sight.

You are EL-OLAM; Everlasting God.

You are JEHOVAH- HOSEENU; Creator.

You are Jehovah NAWKAW; The Lord who strikes.

You are EL SHADDAI; The Lord Almighty.

You are the Lord M'KADDESH; The Lord who sanctifies, that we are made holy.

Come, let us worship and bow down, let us kneel before the Lord our Maker.

*He is our God, and we are the people of His Pasture, and the sheep of His hand.*

Psalm 94:6-7 ASV

No longer are we on the outer courts of salvation. Hear the sound of heaven.

We are no longer called servants. We can enter into the inner court and be called friend.

We can enter in and find rest.

For the inner court is the heart of God. In the heart of God are healing, love, hope and peace.

God is light to the nations and a stalwart fortress. He is a tower of strength and a hiding place. He is the creator of heaven and earth. He is the Redeemer, Deliverer, Shield, Savior and King of Israel. You are the Chief Corner Stone, forever great and mighty.

Why don't you just surrender all? No flesh can glorify in His presence.

Why don't you just enter in? Worship the Lord in the splendor of Holiness.

Fearing the Lord is humility.

Hear the voice of the Father saying, "My son and daughter enter in."

As tears flow down your eyes, look up.

God has given you new priestly garments so that you can enter in.

I will bow down toward your holy temple and will praise your name for your love and your faithfulness, for you have exalted above all things your name and your word. (Psalm 138:2 ESV)

Why don't you press in and come boldly and freely?

*Seeing then We have a great High Priest who passed through the heavens, Jesus the son of God, let us hold fast our confession. For we do not have a High Priest who cannot sympathize with our weakness, but was in all points tempted as we are, yet without sin let us therefore come boldly to the throne of grace to help in time of need.*

Hebrew 4:14-16 ESV

PRESS IN!

Come boldly and freely.

As I enter into the Holies of holies, Lord I slowly approach Your throne silently.

Oh Prince of Peace, as I walk bare footed on Holy ground, I cast my crown down at your feet.

Oh Lord, in Your presence is where I want to be.

Engulfed in Your fire… I come out of the cold of life yearning to be consumed by Your glorious heat.

You are majestic! You are royalty! You are compassion! You are an impressive King! You God do not withhold anything!

*Lord you sit on a throne high and lifted up the train of your robe fills the temple showing nation is defeated. The seraphim cover their eyes and their feet and cry Holy, Holy, Holy, is the Lord God Almighty the earth is filled with your glory.*

Jesus you are *He who sits on the white Horse and is called Faithful and true and in Righteousness. Your eyes are like a flame of fire; your head wore many crowns. Clothed with a robe dipped in blood and Your name is called the Word of God. The armies in heaven, clothed in fine linen, white and cleaned, followed You on a white horse. Your robe has on it thigh King of King and Lord of Lords. You judge and make war. He who sits on the throne makes all things knew for he is the Alpha and the Omega, the Beginning and the End.*

Rev.19:11-16 ESV

Lord, You said the Tabernacle of God is with men and You will dwell with us and we should be Your people.

I want to be the place where You live. Your throne is where I want to live. Sharpen my ear, my eyes, and my tongue. Let the words I speak be a blessing and not a curse. Lord, change my language to a heavenly one.

Abide in my heart. Sit on the couch of my mind, for You are invited in.

I desire for You and I to walk in one accord, like Adam and Eve did in the Garden of Eden.

Salvation, glory, honor and power belong to You.

Lord, for You God are omnipotent and You reign!

You are supreme!

Let Your aroma of sweet cinnamon exude out me.

Clean the impurities out of the water of my spirit.

For too long my circle of influence have been drinking from my well of contaminated water.

In Your presence is fresh water.

She who needs a bath can come freely and she who is thirsty let her drink of Your grace and new mercies.

In Your presence is peace. I kneel and I live as I shout Holy, Holy, and Holy is the Lord God Almighty.

# About the Author

Catherine Ewing-Booker is a native from Milwaukee, Wisconsin. At the age of nine she relocated to Indianapolis, Indiana and lived there until graduating junior College. She currently resides in Evansville, Indiana. She is single with no children as of yet. She finds it a blessing to maximize her singleness being used and stretched by God. Catherine has an associate from Vincennes University and a Bachelor of Social Work Degree from University of Southern Indiana. She is currently working for Harper Elementary school as a Teacher Assistant in an Alternative program, while working on her Masters of Social Work from University of Southern Indiana.

She is a devoted person who loves Jesus Christ. She is a member of The Rock Global Outreach Ministries. She is under the direction of Pastor Lavon and Prophetess Shaneese Dozier. While under their spiritual parental direction, they have entrusted her with her vision to start an after school program called Gideon's Development and Empowerment Ministry. This ministry is for children k-5 grade. The program focuses on education, spiritual and social development.

Catherine loves ministering at the nursing home, evangelizing with those who are lost, and is very passionate about writing what God has given her. In her free time she loves spending time with friends and family. She enjoys traveling, shopping, reading and growing in Jesus Christ.

Contact Catherine Ewing-Booker
at catherine323270@gmail.com
or im_a_gideon@yahoo.com
facebook.com/catherine.ewingbooker